SARA L. WESTON

True North: A Compass for Lesbian Relationships

Contents

Foreword

Love can be beautiful, painful and everything else in between. May your compass always point true North so that you never lose your way. A compass helps you navigate your surroundings when your lost. 'True North' offers a safe passage and the road to the way home.

Preface

Navigating the journey of love, particularly within the context of same-sex relationships, presents its own set of joys, challenges, and intricacies. Drawing inspiration from psychological insights, and the collective wisdom of the Lesbian community, "True North" offers a compass for understanding, fostering, and sustaining healthy and fulfilling lesbian relationships.

1

Chapter 1

1.Understanding Relationship Skills

1.1 The Importance of Relationship Skills

Relationships are an integral part of our lives, shaping our experiences, emotions, and overall well-being. Whether it is a romantic partnership, a friendship, or a familial bond, relationships have the power to bring immense joy, fulfillment, and growth. However, they can also be a source of pain, disappointment, and frustration if we lack the necessary skills to navigate them effectively.

1.1.1 The Impact of Relationships

Relationships play a fundamental role in our lives, influencing our happiness, mental health, and overall quality of life. They provide us with a sense of belonging, support, and connection, allowing us to share our joys, sorrows, and experiences with another person. Research has consistently shown that individuals in healthy and fulfilling relationships tend to have higher levels of life satisfaction, better physical and mental health, and increased longevity.

On the other hand, when relationships are fraught with conflict, miscommunication, and emotional turmoil, they can have detrimental effects on our well-being. Unresolved issues, constant arguments, and a lack of emotional intimacy can lead to feelings of loneliness, stress, and even depression. It is therefore crucial to develop the necessary skills to foster healthy and fulfilling relationships.

1.1.2 The Role of Relationship Skills

Just like any other skill, relationship skills can be learned, practiced, and honed over time. They are the foundation upon which strong and lasting connections are built. Without these skills, relationships can become stagnant, unfulfilling, and prone to conflict.

Relationship skills encompass a wide range of abilities, including effective communication, emotional intelligence, conflict resolution, empathy, and self-awareness. These skills enable individuals to express their needs and desires, listen actively and empathetically, understand and manage their emotions, and navigate conflicts in a constructive manner.

1.1.3 The Benefits of Developing Relationship Skills

Developing relationship skills offers numerous benefits that can positively impact all areas of our lives. By cultivating these skills, we can:

1. Enhance Communication: Effective communication is the cornerstone of any successful relationship. By improving our communication skills, we can express ourselves more clearly, listen attentively, and understand others' perspectives. This fosters mutual understanding, trust, and connection.

2. Build Emotional Intimacy: Emotional intimacy is the deep bond that allows individuals to share their vulnerabilities, fears, and dreams with one another. Developing relationship skills enables us to create a safe and nurturing environment where emotional intimacy can flourish, leading to a deeper connection and a stronger sense of closeness.

3. Resolve Conflicts: Conflict is an inevitable part of any relationship. However, with the right skills, conflicts can be approached as opportunities for growth and understanding rather than sources of tension and resentment. By learning effective conflict resolution strategies, we can navigate disagreements in a respectful and constructive manner, strengthening the relationship in the process.

4. Cultivate Empathy and Compassion: Empathy and compassion are essential qualities that foster understanding, support, and kindness in relationships. By developing these skills, we can better understand and validate the experiences and emotions of our partners, creating a nurturing and empathetic environment.

5. Foster Personal Growth: Relationships provide a unique opportunity for personal growth and self-discovery. By developing relationship skills, we can gain a deeper understanding of ourselves, our needs, and our values. This self-awareness allows us to make conscious choices that align with our authentic selves, leading to personal fulfillment and growth.

In conclusion, relationship skills are vital for creating and maintaining healthy, fulfilling, and lasting connections. By investing in the development of these skills, we can transform our relationships, enhance our well-being, and create a solid foundation for love and happiness. In the following chapters, we will explore various relationship skills and strategies that will empower you to build and sustain the love you desire.

1.2 The Neuroscientific Basis of Relationships

Understanding the neuroscientific basis of relationships can provide valuable insights into the complexities of human connection and help us navigate the challenges that arise in our romantic partnerships. The field of neuroscience has made significant advancements in recent years, shedding light on the intricate workings of the brain and how it influences our behaviors, emotions, and relationships.

1.2.1 The Role of the Brain in Relationships

The brain plays a central role in our experiences of love, attraction, and attachment. Various regions of the brain are involved in processing and regulating emotions, forming social bonds, and maintaining long-term relationships. One of the key areas of interest in relationship neuroscience is the limbic system, which includes structures such as the amygdala, hippocampus, and prefrontal cortex.

The amygdala, often referred to as the emotional center of the brain, is responsible for processing emotions and detecting potential threats or rewards in our environment. It plays a crucial role in our experiences of fear, pleasure, and attraction. When we feel a strong emotional connection with someone, the amygdala is activated, releasing neurotransmitters such as dopamine and oxytocin, which contribute to feelings of pleasure, bonding, and attachment.

The hippocampus, another important structure within the limbic system, is involved in memory formation and retrieval. It helps us remember and recall emotional experiences, including those related to our relationships. This is why we often have vivid memories of significant moments shared with our partners, both positive and negative.

The prefrontal cortex, located at the front of the brain, is responsible for higher-order cognitive functions such as decision-making, self-control, and empathy. It plays a crucial role in regulating our emotions and behaviors within the context of our relationships. When the prefrontal cortex is functioning optimally, we are better equipped to communicate effectively, resolve conflicts, and maintain emotional balance in our relationships.

1.2.2 The Chemistry of Love

Have you ever wondered why you feel a rush of excitement and euphoria when you first meet someone you're attracted to? This intense feeling of infatuation, often referred to as "chemistry," has a neuroscientific basis. When we experience attraction and romantic love, the brain releases a surge of neurotransmitters, including dopamine, norepinephrine, and serotonin.

Dopamine, known as the "pleasure chemical," is associated with feelings of reward and motivation. It creates a sense of anticipation and excitement, making us crave the presence of our romantic partners. Norepinephrine, on the other hand, is responsible for the racing heart, sweaty palms, and heightened arousal commonly experienced during the early stages of love. Serotonin, a neurotransmitter involved in mood regulation, also plays a role in romantic love, contributing to feelings of happiness and contentment.

These neurochemical reactions in the brain create a powerful cocktail of emotions that can make us feel deeply connected and infatuated with our partners. However, it's important to note that this initial surge of chemistry is not sustainable in the long term. As the relationship progresses, the brain's response to our partners evolves, and other factors such as emotional intimacy and shared experiences become more important in maintaining a lasting bond.

1.2.3 Attachment and Bonding

Attachment theory, developed by psychologist John Bowlby, provides valuable insights into how our early experiences with caregivers shape our attachment styles and influence our adult relationships. The attachment system, which is deeply rooted in the brain, seeks to establish and maintain close emotional bonds with others.

Secure attachment, characterized by a sense of trust, safety, and comfort in relationships, is associated with positive outcomes in romantic partnerships. In contrast, insecure attachment styles, such as anxious or avoidant attachment, can lead to difficulties in forming and maintaining healthy relationships.

Neuroscience research has shown that the quality of our early attachments influences the development of neural pathways related to social bonding and emotional regulation. For example, individuals with secure attachment styles tend to have a well-developed prefrontal cortex, enabling them to regulate their emotions effectively and engage in healthy relationship behaviors. On the other hand, those with insecure attachment styles may exhibit heightened reactivity in the amygdala, leading to difficulties in managing emotions and navigating relationship challenges.

1.2.4 The Impact of Relationship Skills on the Brain

The brain is highly adaptable and capable of change throughout our lives. This phenomenon, known as neuroplasticity, means that we can develop and strengthen relationship skills that positively impact our brain's functioning and enhance our romantic partnerships.

Research has shown that practicing skills such as effective communication, empathy, and conflict resolution can lead to structural and functional changes in the brain. For example, engaging in active listening and validation exercises can strengthen neural pathways associated with empathy and emotional attunement. Similarly, learning and implementing nonviolent communication techniques can promote healthier patterns of interaction and reduce the activation of stress response systems in the brain.

By actively developing relationship skills, we can create new neural pathways that support healthier relationship dynamics and enhance our overall well-being. These skills not only improve the quality of our current relationships but also lay the foundation for future connections.

In the following chapters, we will explore various relationship skills and strategies that can help you build and maintain lasting love. By understanding the neuroscientific basis of relationships and applying these skills, you can create a strong foundation for a fulfilling and harmonious partnership. Remember, relationships require effort and continuous growth, but with the right skills, they can become a source of joy, support, and personal transformation.

1.3 Common Challenges in Relationships

Relationships can be incredibly rewarding and fulfilling, but they can also be challenging and complex. It is important to recognize that common challenges often arise in relationships, regardless of sexual orientation or gender identity. In this section, we will explore some of these challenges and provide insights on how to navigate them effectively.

1.3.1 Communication Issues

One of the most common challenges in relationships is communication. Effective communication is the foundation of a healthy and thriving partnership. However, miscommunication, misunderstandings, and lack of effective listening can lead to conflicts and emotional distance.

To overcome communication issues, it is crucial to cultivate active listening skills and practice open and honest communication. This involves actively listening to your partner's thoughts and feelings without interrupting or judging. It also means expressing yourself clearly and respectfully, using "I" statements to convey your needs and desires.

1.3.2 Conflict Resolution

Conflict is a natural part of any relationship, and how it is handled can greatly impact the overall health and longevity of the partnership. Many couples struggle with finding constructive ways to resolve conflicts, often resorting to unhealthy patterns such as avoidance, aggression, or passive-aggressive behavior.

Learning effective conflict resolution strategies can help couples navigate disagreements in a healthy and productive manner. This includes learning to express emotions without blame or criticism, actively seeking understanding, and finding mutually beneficial solutions. It is important to approach conflicts as opportunities for growth and understanding rather than as threats to the relationship.

1.3.3 Trust and Betrayal

Trust is the cornerstone of any successful relationship. However, building and maintaining trust can be challenging, especially if one or both partners have experienced past betrayals or have trust issues. Trust can be eroded by dishonesty, infidelity, or broken promises.

Rebuilding trust after a betrayal requires open and honest communication, transparency, and consistent actions that demonstrate trustworthiness. It also requires patience and understanding from both partners. It is essential to address the underlying issues that led to the betrayal and work together to establish new patterns of trust and security.

1.3.4 Balancing Independence and Togetherness

Finding the right balance between independence and togetherness is another common challenge in relationships. It is important for each partner to maintain their individuality, pursue their own interests, and have a sense of autonomy. However, too much independence can lead to emotional distance and a lack of connection.

On the other hand, excessive togetherness can result in codependency and a loss of personal identity. Striking a healthy balance requires open communication, mutual respect, and a willingness to support each other's individual growth and passions while nurturing the bond between partners.

1.3.5 Life Transitions and External Pressures

Life is full of transitions, both big and small, that can put strain on a relationship. These transitions may include career changes, moving to a new city, starting a family, or dealing with the loss of a loved one. Additionally, external pressures such as financial stress, societal expectations, or cultural differences can also impact a relationship.

Navigating these challenges requires open and honest communication, empathy, and a willingness to adapt and support each other through the ups and downs of life. It is important to recognize that these transitions and external pressures can be opportunities for growth and strengthening the bond between partners.

1.3.6 Emotional Intimacy and Sexual Connection

Maintaining emotional intimacy and a satisfying sexual connection is vital for a healthy and fulfilling relationship. However, many couples struggle with maintaining these aspects over time. Stress, fatigue, and the demands of daily life can take a toll on emotional and sexual intimacy.

To nurture emotional intimacy, it is important to create a safe and supportive environment where both partners can express their feelings and vulnerabilities. This involves active listening, empathy, and regular emotional check-ins. Similarly, fostering a satisfying sexual connection requires open communication, exploration of desires and fantasies, and a willingness to prioritize intimacy in the relationship.

Navigating these common challenges in relationships requires dedication, effort, and a commitment to personal growth. By developing the necessary skills and adopting a proactive approach, couples can overcome these challenges and build a strong foundation for lasting love. In the following chapters, we will delve deeper into these skills and provide practical strategies for cultivating a thriving and fulfilling relationship.

1.4 The Benefits of Developing Relationship Skills

Developing relationship skills can have numerous benefits that can greatly enhance your personal and romantic life. Whether you have experienced heartbreak and disillusionment in the past or are simply looking to improve your current relationship, investing in the development of these skills can lead to a more fulfilling and lasting love.

1.4.1 Building Strong Foundations

One of the key benefits of developing relationship skills is the ability to build a strong foundation for your relationship. By understanding the importance of trust, honesty, and effective communication, you can establish a solid base upon which your relationship can thrive. These skills allow you to navigate challenges and conflicts with greater ease, fostering a sense of security and stability in your partnership.

1.4.2 Enhancing Emotional Connection

Another significant benefit of honing your relationship skills is the ability to deepen emotional connection with your partner. By developing emotional intelligence and cultivating empathy and compassion, you can better understand and respond to your partner's needs and emotions. This heightened emotional connection fosters a sense of intimacy and closeness, allowing you to truly connect on a deeper level.

1.4.3 Effective Conflict Resolution

Conflict is an inevitable part of any relationship, but having the skills to effectively resolve conflicts can make a significant difference in the longevity and happiness of your partnership. By learning conflict resolution strategies and practicing active listening and validation, you can navigate disagreements in a healthy and constructive manner. This not only strengthens your bond but also allows for personal growth and understanding within the relationship.

1.4.4 Improved Communication

Developing relationship skills also leads to improved communication, which is the cornerstone of any successful partnership. Effective communication involves not only expressing your needs and desires but also actively listening to your partner and validating their experiences. By mastering these skills, you can avoid misunderstandings, build trust, and foster a sense of mutual respect and understanding.

1.4.5 Increased Self-Awareness and Personal Growth

Investing in the development of relationship skills also promotes personal growth and self-awareness. By engaging in self-reflection and cultivating emotional intelligence, you gain a deeper understanding of your own needs, values, and triggers. This self-awareness allows you to take responsibility for your actions and emotions, leading to personal growth and a healthier approach to relationships.

1.4.6 Greater Relationship Satisfaction

Ultimately, the benefits of developing relationship skills culminate in greater relationship satisfaction. By investing time and effort into learning and practicing these skills, you can create a relationship that is fulfilling, harmonious, and long-lasting. The ability to navigate challenges, communicate effectively, and foster emotional connection leads to a deeper sense of happiness and contentment within your partnership.

1.4.7 Improved Overall Well-being

In addition to the benefits within the realm of relationships, developing these skills can also have a positive impact on your overall well-being. Healthy and fulfilling relationships contribute to increased happiness, reduced stress levels, and improved mental and emotional health. By investing in the development of relationship skills, you are not only enhancing your romantic life but also promoting your overall happiness and well-being.

In conclusion, developing relationship skills offers a multitude of benefits that can greatly enhance your personal and romantic life. From building strong foundations and enhancing emotional connection to improving communication and fostering personal growth, these skills are essential for creating and maintaining a happy, healthy, and lasting relationship. By investing in the development of these skills, you are taking a proactive step towards creating the love and connection you desire and deserve.

2

Chapter 2

2. Finding the Right Person

2.1 Identifying Your Relationship Needs and Values

In order to find the right person and build a lasting love, it is essential to first identify your relationship needs and values. Understanding what you truly desire and require in a partner will guide you towards creating a fulfilling and compatible relationship.

2.1.1 Reflecting on Your Relationship Needs

Take some time for self-reflection and introspection to gain clarity on your relationship needs. Consider the following questions:

1. What are your core values and beliefs? What values do you seek in a partner?
2. What are your emotional needs? How do you want to feel in a relationship?
3. What are your long-term goals and aspirations? How do you envision your ideal future with a partner?

4. What are your deal-breakers? What are the qualities or behaviors that you cannot tolerate in a relationship?

5. What are your communication and intimacy preferences? How do you express and receive love?

By answering these questions honestly, you will gain a deeper understanding of your own desires and requirements in a relationship. This self-awareness will serve as a compass to guide you towards finding a partner who aligns with your values and can meet your needs.

2.1.2 Defining Your Relationship Values

Relationship values are the guiding principles that shape the dynamics and foundation of a partnership. They are the fundamental beliefs and qualities that you prioritize in a relationship. Identifying your relationship values will help you attract a partner who shares similar values and create a strong and harmonious connection.

Consider the following relationship values and reflect on which ones resonate with you:

1. Trust: Trust is the foundation of any healthy relationship. It involves having faith in your partner's honesty, reliability, and intentions.

2. Communication: Open and effective communication is vital for understanding, resolving conflicts, and building emotional intimacy.

3. Respect: Mutual respect involves valuing each other's opinions, boundaries, and autonomy.

4. Emotional Support: Emotional support entails being there for each other during both the highs and lows, providing comfort, empathy, and understanding.

5. Growth and Development: A relationship that encourages personal growth and supports each other's aspirations and dreams.

6. Equality and Partnership: A relationship built on equality, where both partners contribute, make decisions together, and share responsibilities.

7. Intimacy: Physical and emotional intimacy, including affection, sexual connection, and deep emotional bonds.

8. Fun and Adventure: A relationship that embraces joy, spontaneity, and shared experiences.

9. Loyalty and Commitment: A commitment to being faithful, dedicated, and loyal to each other.

These are just a few examples of relationship values, and it's important to identify the values that resonate with you personally. Once you have a clear understanding of your relationship values, you can use them as a guide when evaluating potential partners and building a strong foundation for your relationship.

2.1.3 Assessing Compatibility

Once you have identified your relationship needs and values, it is crucial to assess the compatibility between you and a potential partner. Compatibility goes beyond surface-level attraction and involves aligning on important aspects of life, values, and goals.

Consider the following factors when assessing compatibility:

1. Shared Values: Do your values align? Are you both seeking similar things in a relationship and life?

2. Communication Style: Do you communicate effectively and understand each other's needs and perspectives?

3. Emotional Connection: Do you feel a deep emotional connection and understanding with each other?

4. Interests and Hobbies: Do you share common interests and enjoy spending time together?

5. Future Goals: Do your long-term goals and aspirations align? Can you support each other's dreams?

6. Conflict Resolution: How do you handle conflicts? Are you able to resolve disagreements in a healthy and respectful manner?

7. Intimacy and Chemistry: Is there a strong physical and emotional connection between you?

Assessing compatibility requires open and honest communication, observation, and spending quality time together. It is important to remember that no relationship is perfect, and some differences can be worked through with effective communication and compromise. However, it is crucial to ensure that your core needs and values align for a fulfilling and lasting partnership.

By identifying your relationship needs and values and assessing compatibility, you will be better equipped to find a partner who is a true match for you. Remember, building a lasting love starts with understanding yourself and what you truly desire in a relationship.

2.2 Recognizing Red Flags in Potential Partners

When it comes to finding the right person, it is essential to be able to recognize red flags in potential partners. Red flags are warning signs that indicate potential issues or challenges in a relationship. While it is important to approach new relationships with an open mind and heart, it is equally important to be aware of these red flags to protect yourself from potential harm or heartbreak.

2.2.1 Lack of Communication and Emotional Availability

One of the most significant red flags in a potential partner is a lack of communication and emotional availability. Healthy relationships thrive on open and honest communication, where both partners feel comfortable expressing their thoughts, feelings, and needs. If you notice that your potential partner struggles to communicate effectively or seems emotionally distant, it may be a sign that they are not ready or capable of building a deep emotional connection.

2.2.2 Disrespectful or Controlling Behavior

Respect is the foundation of any healthy relationship. If you observe disrespectful or controlling behavior in a potential partner, it is crucial to take it seriously. Red flags in this area can include belittling or demeaning comments, attempts to control your actions or decisions, or a lack of respect for your boundaries and autonomy. Remember, a healthy relationship should be built on mutual respect and equality.

2.2.3 Inconsistent or Unreliable Behavior

Consistency and reliability are essential qualities in a potential partner. If you notice that the person you are dating frequently cancels plans, is often late, or fails to follow through on their commitments, it may be a red flag indicating a lack of reliability. Trust is a vital component of a successful relationship, and inconsistent or unreliable behavior can erode that trust over time.

2.2.4 Lack of Accountability and Responsibility

A healthy relationship requires both partners to take accountability for their actions and accept responsibility for their mistakes. If you find that your potential partner consistently blames others for their problems, avoids taking responsibility for their actions, or refuses to apologize when they have done something wrong, it may be a red flag indicating a lack of maturity and emotional growth.

2.2.5 Unresolved Emotional Baggage or Trauma

We all carry emotional baggage from our past, but it is essential to be aware of how it may impact a potential relationship. If your potential partner has unresolved trauma or emotional baggage that they have not addressed or worked through, it can significantly affect the dynamics of your relationship. It is crucial to have open and honest conversations about past experiences and ensure that both partners are committed to personal growth and healing.

2.2.6 Lack of Shared Values and Goals

While differences can enrich a relationship, it is important to have shared values and goals with your potential partner. If you find that your values and goals are fundamentally incompatible, it may be a red flag indicating potential challenges in the future. It is essential to have open and honest conversations about your aspirations, beliefs, and values to ensure that you are on the same page and can support each other's growth and happiness.

2.2.7 Patterns of Disloyalty or Infidelity

Trust is the cornerstone of any successful relationship, and patterns of disloyalty or infidelity should not be taken lightly. If you discover that your potential partner has a history of cheating or has been unfaithful in past relationships, it is crucial to consider whether you can trust them fully. While people can change and grow, it is essential to have open and honest conversations about trust and fidelity to ensure that both partners are committed to building a faithful and monogamous relationship.

Recognizing these red flags in potential partners is essential for protecting yourself and ensuring that you enter into a healthy and fulfilling relationship. It is important to trust your instincts and not ignore any warning signs that may arise. Remember, finding the right person involves not only recognizing the qualities you desire but also being aware of the potential challenges that may arise. By being mindful of these red flags, you can make informed decisions and increase your chances of finding a lasting and loving partnership.

2.3 Effective Communication in Dating

Effective communication is a crucial skill in dating that can make or break a potential relationship. It is through communication that we get to know each other, express our needs and desires, and build a strong foundation of understanding and connection. In the early stages of dating, effective communication sets the stage for a healthy and fulfilling relationship.

2.3.1 Active Listening and Empathy

One of the key aspects of effective communication in dating is active listening. Active listening involves fully engaging with your partner's words, thoughts, and emotions. It means giving them your full attention, maintaining eye contact, and showing genuine interest in what they have to say. By actively listening, you demonstrate that you value their perspective and are willing to understand them on a deeper level.

Empathy is closely tied to active listening and is an essential component of effective communication. It involves putting yourself in your partner's shoes and trying to understand their feelings and experiences. By practicing empathy, you create a safe and supportive environment where your partner feels heard and understood. This fosters a sense of emotional connection and trust, which is vital for a successful relationship.

2.3.2 Expressing Needs and Desires

In addition to listening and understanding, it is equally important to express your own needs and desires in a dating relationship. Open and honest communication about what you want and expect from the relationship allows both partners to align their expectations and work towards a common goal. It is essential to communicate your boundaries, values, and non-negotiables early on to ensure compatibility and avoid misunderstandings later.

When expressing your needs and desires, it is crucial to do so in a respectful and non-confrontational manner. Using "I" statements instead of "you" statements can help avoid blame and defensiveness. For example, saying "I feel" or "I need" instead of "You always" or "You never" can create a more constructive and open dialogue. Remember, effective communication is about finding a balance between expressing yourself and being receptive to your partner's needs as well.

2.3.3 Nonviolent Communication Techniques

Nonviolent communication techniques can be particularly helpful in dating situations where emotions may run high or conflicts may arise. This approach, developed by Marshall Rosenberg, focuses on expressing oneself honestly while also empathetically listening to the other person's feelings and needs. Nonviolent communication encourages open dialogue, understanding, and finding mutually beneficial solutions.

One of the key principles of nonviolent communication is to separate observations from evaluations. Instead of making judgments or assumptions, focus on describing the specific behaviors or situations that are causing concern. This helps to avoid blame and defensiveness and allows for a more productive conversation.

Another important aspect of nonviolent communication is expressing feelings and needs rather than making demands. By clearly articulating your emotions and underlying needs, you create an opportunity for your partner to understand and respond to them. This approach fosters empathy and cooperation, leading to more effective problem-solving and conflict resolution.

2.3.4 Conflict Resolution Strategies

Conflict is a natural part of any relationship, including dating relationships. However, how conflicts are handled can significantly impact the health and longevity of the relationship. Effective communication in dating involves learning and implementing conflict resolution strategies that promote understanding, compromise, and growth.

One important strategy is to approach conflicts with a mindset of collaboration rather than competition. Instead of viewing the conflict as a win-lose situation, strive for a win-win outcome where both partners' needs are considered and respected. This requires active listening, empathy, and a willingness to find mutually beneficial solutions.

Another valuable technique is to take breaks when conflicts become heated or overwhelming. Sometimes, stepping away from the situation temporarily can help both partners calm down and gain perspective. It is essential to establish boundaries and agree on a time to reconvene and continue the discussion in a more constructive manner.

Lastly, practicing forgiveness and letting go of grudges is crucial for effective conflict resolution. Holding onto past grievances can hinder the growth and progress of the relationship. By cultivating forgiveness and focusing on finding solutions rather than dwelling on past mistakes, you create a space for healing and growth.

In conclusion, effective communication in dating is the foundation for building a healthy and lasting relationship. By actively listening, expressing needs and desires, utilizing nonviolent communication techniques, and implementing conflict resolution strategies, you can create a strong and meaningful connection with your partner. Remember, communication is a skill that can be learned and improved upon, and investing in developing these skills will greatly enhance your dating experiences and increase the likelihood of finding a compatible and fulfilling long-term partner.

2.4 Building Emotional Connection and Chemistry

Building emotional connection and chemistry is a crucial aspect of any successful and fulfilling relationship. It is the foundation upon which love and intimacy thrive. Without a strong emotional connection, a relationship can feel shallow and lacking in depth. In this section, we will explore the importance of building emotional connection and chemistry and provide practical strategies to cultivate and nurture these essential elements.

2.4.1 Understanding Emotional Connection

Emotional connection refers to the deep bond and understanding that develops between two individuals. It involves the ability to empathize, communicate, and share vulnerable aspects of oneself with a partner. Emotional connection is the glue that holds relationships together, allowing couples to weather storms and navigate challenges with resilience.

To build emotional connection, it is essential to cultivate open and honest communication. This involves actively listening to your partner, validating their feelings, and expressing empathy and understanding. By creating a safe space for vulnerability and emotional expression, you can foster a deeper sense of connection and intimacy.

2.4.2 Cultivating Emotional Intimacy

Emotional intimacy goes hand in hand with emotional connection. It involves sharing your innermost thoughts, fears, dreams, and desires with your partner. Emotional intimacy allows for a deeper level of understanding and acceptance, fostering a sense of closeness and trust.

To cultivate emotional intimacy, it is crucial to create opportunities for meaningful conversations. Set aside dedicated time to connect with your partner on a deeper level. This can involve engaging in activities that promote emotional sharing, such as taking walks together, having regular date nights, or engaging in deep conversations about your hopes and aspirations.

2.4.3 Building Trust and Vulnerability

Trust is the cornerstone of any healthy and lasting relationship. Without trust, it is challenging to build emotional connection and chemistry. Trust involves being reliable, honest, and transparent with your partner. It requires vulnerability and the willingness to share your authentic self.

To build trust, it is important to follow through on your commitments and be consistent in your actions. Communicate openly and honestly, and be willing to address any concerns or insecurities that may arise. By demonstrating trustworthiness and vulnerability, you create a safe space for your partner to do the same, deepening the emotional connection between you.

2.4.4 Nurturing Physical and Emotional Chemistry

Chemistry is often described as the spark or magnetic attraction between two individuals. It encompasses both physical and emotional aspects of a relationship. While chemistry can be present from the beginning, it also requires effort and nurturing to sustain over time.

To nurture physical chemistry, it is important to prioritize physical affection and intimacy. This can involve engaging in activities that promote closeness, such as cuddling, holding hands, or engaging in shared hobbies. Additionally, maintaining a healthy and active lifestyle can contribute to increased physical attraction and energy.

Emotional chemistry, on the other hand, is nurtured through emotional connection and understanding. It involves being attuned to your partner's needs, desires, and emotions. By actively listening, validating, and supporting each other, you can deepen the emotional bond and create a strong foundation for lasting love.

2.4.5 Cultivating Shared Experiences

Shared experiences play a vital role in building emotional connection and chemistry. Engaging in activities together allows couples to create lasting memories, strengthen their bond, and deepen their understanding of each other.

To cultivate shared experiences, it is important to prioritize quality time together. This can involve planning regular date nights, taking vacations, or engaging in shared hobbies and interests. By actively participating in each other's lives and creating new experiences together, you can foster a sense of adventure and connection.

2.4.6 Honoring Individuality within the Relationship

While building emotional connection and chemistry is crucial, it is equally important to honor and respect each other's individuality within the relationship. Each partner brings their unique strengths, interests, and perspectives, which should be celebrated and nurtured.

To honor individuality, it is important to create space for personal growth and self-expression. Encourage each other to pursue individual passions and hobbies, and support each other's personal goals and aspirations. By fostering a sense of independence and autonomy within the relationship, you can enhance the emotional connection and create a healthy balance between togetherness and individuality.

In conclusion, building emotional connection and chemistry is a fundamental aspect of creating a lasting and fulfilling relationship. By cultivating open communication, trust, vulnerability, and shared experiences, you can deepen the emotional bond and create a strong foundation for love to thrive. Remember, building emotional connection and chemistry requires effort and commitment from both partners, but the rewards are immeasurable.

3

Chapter 3

3.Becoming the Right Person

3.1 Self-Reflection and Personal Growth

Self-reflection and personal growth are essential components of becoming the right person for a lasting and fulfilling relationship. In order to build a strong foundation with someone else, it is crucial to first understand and develop ourselves. This chapter will explore the importance of self-reflection and personal growth in the context of relationships, and provide practical strategies for cultivating these qualities.

3.1.1 Understanding the Importance of Self-Reflection

Self-reflection is the process of introspection and examination of one's thoughts, emotions, and behaviors. It involves taking a step back from our daily lives and relationships to gain a deeper understanding of ourselves. By engaging in self-reflection, we can identify our strengths, weaknesses, values, and desires. This self-awareness allows us to make conscious choices and take intentional actions that align with our authentic selves.

In the context of relationships, self-reflection is crucial because it helps us understand our patterns, triggers, and needs. It allows us to identify any unresolved emotional wounds or limiting beliefs that may be impacting our ability to connect with others. By gaining insight into ourselves, we can break free from destructive patterns and create healthier dynamics in our relationships.

3.1.2 The Power of Personal Growth

Personal growth refers to the continuous process of self-improvement and development. It involves actively seeking opportunities for learning, expanding our perspectives, and challenging ourselves to become the best versions of ourselves. Personal growth is a lifelong journey that requires openness, curiosity, and a willingness to step outside of our comfort zones.

In the context of relationships, personal growth is essential because it allows us to evolve and adapt as individuals. As we grow and change, our needs and desires may shift, and it is important to communicate these changes to our partners. Personal growth also enables us to develop the emotional intelligence, self-confidence, and empathy necessary for building and maintaining healthy relationships.

3.1.3 Cultivating Self-Reflection and Personal Growth

1. **Practice mindfulness**: Mindfulness involves being fully present in the moment and non-judgmentally observing our thoughts, emotions, and sensations. By practicing mindfulness, we can develop a greater awareness of ourselves and our reactions to different situations. This awareness allows us to respond consciously rather than react impulsively, leading to healthier interactions with others.
2. **Journaling**: Writing in a journal can be a powerful tool for self-reflection. Take time each day to write about your thoughts, feelings, and experiences. Use this space to explore your emotions, identify patterns, and gain clarity on your values and goals. Journaling can also serve as a means of self-expression and a way to process challenging emotions.

3. **Seek feedback**: Ask trusted friends, family members, or mentors for feedback on your strengths and areas for growth. Sometimes, others can provide valuable insights that we may not see ourselves. Be open to receiving constructive criticism and use it as an opportunity for personal growth.

4. **Engage in therapy or coaching**: Working with a therapist or coach can provide a supportive and structured environment for self-reflection and personal growth. These professionals can help you explore your past experiences, identify patterns, and develop strategies for personal development. They can also provide guidance and support as you navigate the challenges and transitions in your relationships.

5. **Embrace lifelong learning**: Commit to continuous learning and growth by seeking out books, workshops, courses, or seminars that align with your interests and goals. Engaging in learning opportunities can expand your knowledge, challenge your perspectives, and inspire personal growth.

3.1.4 Embracing Self-Reflection and Personal Growth for Lasting Love

Self-reflection and personal growth are not one-time tasks but ongoing practices that contribute to the development of a strong and fulfilling relationship. By understanding ourselves, cultivating self-awareness, and actively working on personal growth, we become better equipped to navigate the complexities of relationships.

Remember, becoming the right person for a lasting love requires a commitment to self-reflection and personal growth. Embrace the journey of self-discovery, and you will not only enhance your own well-being but also create the foundation for a healthy and thriving relationship.

3.2 Developing Emotional Intelligence

Emotional intelligence is a crucial aspect of personal growth and plays a significant role in developing and maintaining healthy relationships. It involves the ability to recognize, understand, and manage our own emotions, as well as the emotions of others. By cultivating emotional intelligence, we can enhance our communication skills, build stronger connections, and navigate conflicts more effectively.

3.2.1 Understanding Emotional Intelligence

Emotional intelligence encompasses various skills and competencies that contribute to our overall emotional well-being and relationship success. These skills include self-awareness, self-regulation, empathy, and effective communication. Let's explore each of these components in more detail:

Self-Awareness

Self-awareness is the foundation of emotional intelligence. It involves being in tune with our own emotions, thoughts, and behaviors. By developing self-awareness, we can gain a deeper understanding of our strengths, weaknesses, values, and triggers. This awareness allows us to make conscious choices and respond to situations in a more intentional and authentic manner.

To enhance self-awareness, it is essential to practice self-reflection regularly. This can involve journaling, meditation, or seeking feedback from trusted friends or therapists. By examining our emotions and patterns of behavior, we can identify areas for growth and make positive changes in our lives and relationships.

Self-Regulation

Self-regulation refers to the ability to manage and control our emotions, impulses, and reactions. It involves finding healthy ways to express and channel our emotions, rather than allowing them to dictate our behavior. Developing self-regulation skills allows us to respond to challenging situations with composure and thoughtfulness, rather than reacting impulsively.

To cultivate self-regulation, it is important to practice self-care and stress management techniques. This can include engaging in activities that promote relaxation and emotional well-being, such as exercise, mindfulness, or engaging in hobbies. By taking care of our own emotional needs, we can better regulate our emotions and navigate conflicts in a more constructive manner.

Empathy

Empathy is the ability to understand and share the feelings of others. It involves putting ourselves in someone else's shoes and recognizing their emotions and perspectives. Developing empathy allows us to connect with others on a deeper level, validate their experiences, and respond with compassion and understanding.

To enhance empathy, it is crucial to practice active listening and observation. This involves paying attention to verbal and nonverbal cues, asking open-ended questions, and genuinely seeking to understand the other person's point of view. By practicing empathy, we can foster stronger connections and create a safe and supportive environment for our partners.

Effective Communication

Effective communication is a vital component of emotional intelligence. It involves expressing ourselves clearly and assertively, while also actively listening to others. By improving our communication skills, we can avoid misunderstandings, resolve conflicts, and build trust and intimacy in our relationships.

To enhance communication, it is important to practice active listening, validation, and assertiveness. This includes giving our full attention to the speaker, paraphrasing their words to ensure understanding, and expressing our needs and desires in a respectful and assertive manner. By fostering open and honest communication, we can create a foundation of trust and understanding in our relationships.

3.2.2 Developing Emotional Intelligence in Relationships

Developing emotional intelligence is an ongoing process that requires self-reflection, practice, and a willingness to grow. Here are some strategies to help you develop emotional intelligence in your relationships:

1. Self-Reflection

Take time to reflect on your emotions, thoughts, and behaviors. Consider how they impact your relationships and identify areas for improvement. Journaling, therapy, or seeking feedback from trusted individuals can be helpful in gaining self-awareness and understanding your emotional patterns.

2. Practice Mindfulness

Engage in mindfulness practices to cultivate self-awareness and regulate your emotions. Mindfulness involves being fully present in the moment, observing your thoughts and emotions without judgment. This practice can help you become more attuned to your own emotions and respond to them in a more intentional and constructive manner.

3. Seek Feedback

Ask for feedback from your partner or trusted friends about how you show up in your relationships. Be open to constructive criticism and use it as an opportunity for growth. Feedback can provide valuable insights into your blind spots and help you develop a deeper understanding of yourself and your impact on others.

4. Develop Empathy

Practice putting yourself in your partner's shoes and genuinely seeking to understand their emotions and perspectives. Engage in active listening, validate their experiences, and respond with empathy and compassion. By developing empathy, you can foster deeper connections and create a safe and supportive environment in your relationships.

5. Improve Communication Skills

Enhance your communication skills by practicing active listening, validation, and assertiveness. Give your full attention to the speaker, paraphrase their words to ensure understanding, and express your needs and desires in a respectful and assertive manner. Effective communication is essential for building trust, resolving conflicts, and fostering intimacy in your relationships.

Remember, developing emotional intelligence is a lifelong journey. It requires patience, self-compassion, and a commitment to personal growth. By cultivating emotional intelligence, you can enhance your relationships, create deeper connections, and experience lasting love and fulfillment.

3.3 Building Self-Confidence and Self-Worth

Building self-confidence and self-worth is a crucial aspect of becoming the right person for a lasting and fulfilling relationship. When you possess a strong sense of self and believe in your own worth, you are better equipped to navigate the ups and downs of a partnership with grace and resilience. In this section, we will explore the importance of building self-confidence and self-worth and provide practical strategies to help you cultivate these qualities.

3.3.1 Understanding Self-Confidence

Self-confidence is the belief in your own abilities, qualities, and worth. It is an inner strength that allows you to trust yourself and your decisions. When you have self-confidence, you are more likely to take risks, assert your needs and boundaries, and communicate effectively in your relationships. It is important to note that self-confidence is not about being perfect or having all the answers. It is about embracing your strengths and accepting your imperfections.

3.3.2 Recognizing the Importance of Self-Worth

Self-worth is closely tied to self-confidence and refers to the value and respect you have for yourself. It is the belief that you are deserving of love, respect, and happiness. When you have a healthy sense of self-worth, you are less likely to settle for less than you deserve in a relationship. You understand your own needs and are able to prioritize your well-being. Cultivating self-worth is essential for creating and maintaining healthy boundaries, as well as for attracting and sustaining a loving and respectful partnership.

3.3.3 Building Self-Confidence

Building self-confidence is a process that requires self-reflection, self-compassion, and practice. Here are some strategies to help you boost your self-confidence:

1. Self-Reflection and Self-Awareness

Take the time to reflect on your strengths, accomplishments, and positive qualities. Write them down and remind yourself of them regularly. Acknowledge your achievements, no matter how small they may seem. This practice will help you develop a more positive and realistic self-perception.

2. Challenging Negative Self-Talk

Pay attention to your inner dialogue and challenge any negative thoughts or self-doubt. Replace self-criticism with self-compassion and affirmations. Remind yourself of your worth and capabilities. Surround yourself with positive and supportive people who uplift and encourage you.

3. Setting and Achieving Goals

Setting and achieving goals can significantly boost your self-confidence. Start with small, attainable goals and gradually work your way up to more challenging ones. Celebrate your accomplishments along the way, as each success will reinforce your belief in your abilities.

4. Stepping Outside Your Comfort Zone

Pushing yourself outside of your comfort zone can be intimidating but is essential for personal growth and building self-confidence. Take on new challenges, try new activities, and embrace opportunities for learning and self-improvement. Each time you step outside your comfort zone and succeed, your self-confidence will grow.

3.3.4 Cultivating Self-Worth

Cultivating self-worth is an ongoing practice that involves nurturing a positive self-image and prioritizing self-care. Here are some strategies to help you cultivate self-worth:

1. Practicing Self-Compassion

Be kind and compassionate towards yourself. Treat yourself with the same love and care you would offer to a dear friend. Practice self-acceptance and forgiveness, recognizing that everyone makes mistakes and has flaws. Embrace your uniqueness and celebrate your individuality.

2. Setting Boundaries

Setting and maintaining healthy boundaries is crucial for cultivating self-worth. Clearly communicate your needs, desires, and limits to others. Learn to say no when necessary and prioritize your well-being. Respect yourself enough to walk away from relationships or situations that do not align with your values and needs.

3. Engaging in Self-Care

Make self-care a priority in your life. Take time to engage in activities that bring you joy, relaxation, and fulfillment. Nurture your physical, emotional, and mental well-being. Practice self-care rituals such as exercise, meditation, journaling, or spending time in nature. Prioritizing self-care sends a powerful message to yourself and others that you value and prioritize your own needs.

4. Surrounding Yourself with Positive Influences

Surround yourself with people who uplift and support you. Seek out relationships and friendships that are built on mutual respect, love, and encouragement. Distance yourself from toxic individuals who undermine your self-worth. Surrounding yourself with positive influences will reinforce your belief in your own value and worthiness of love.

Remember, building self-confidence and self-worth is a journey that takes time and effort. Be patient with yourself and celebrate each step forward. As you cultivate these qualities, you will become the right person not only for a lasting and loving relationship but also for a fulfilling and joyful life.

3.4 Cultivating Empathy and Compassion

Empathy and compassion are essential qualities for building and maintaining a healthy and lasting relationship. These qualities allow you to understand and connect with your partner on a deeper level, fostering trust, intimacy, and emotional support. In this section, we will explore the importance of cultivating empathy and compassion in your relationship and provide practical strategies to develop these qualities.

The Power of Empathy

Empathy is the ability to understand and share the feelings of another person. It involves putting yourself in your partner's shoes and truly experiencing their emotions. When you practice empathy, you create a safe and supportive space for your partner to express themselves without fear of judgment or rejection. This deep level of understanding strengthens the emotional bond between you and promotes open and honest communication.

To cultivate empathy in your relationship, start by actively listening to your partner. Pay attention to their verbal and nonverbal cues, and try to understand their perspective without interrupting or jumping to conclusions. Validate their feelings by acknowledging and accepting them, even if you may not fully agree or understand at first. Show genuine interest in their experiences and ask open-ended questions to encourage them to share more.

Another powerful way to develop empathy is through self-reflection. Take the time to examine your own emotions and experiences, as this will help you relate to and empathize with your partner's feelings. Practice self-compassion and treat yourself with kindness and understanding, as this will enable you to extend the same compassion to your partner.

The Importance of Compassion

Compassion goes hand in hand with empathy and involves a genuine concern for your partner's well-being. It is the willingness to offer support, understanding, and kindness, especially during challenging times. When you cultivate compassion in your relationship, you create a nurturing and loving environment where both partners feel valued and cared for.

To develop compassion, start by practicing kindness towards yourself and your partner. Be patient and understanding with each other's flaws and imperfections, recognizing that everyone makes mistakes and has their own struggles. Offer words of encouragement and acts of kindness to uplift and support your partner, especially when they are going through difficult times.

Compassion also involves being present and attentive to your partner's needs. Take the time to actively listen and respond with empathy when they express their concerns or share their experiences. Show genuine interest in their well-being and offer your support and assistance whenever possible. Small gestures of compassion, such as preparing their favorite meal or offering a comforting hug, can go a long way in strengthening your connection.

Cultivating Empathy and Compassion Together

Building empathy and compassion in your relationship requires effort and intention from both partners. It is a collaborative process that involves open communication, mutual understanding, and a willingness to grow together. Here are some strategies to cultivate empathy and compassion together:

1. Practice active listening: Make a conscious effort to listen attentively to your partner without interrupting or judging. Show genuine interest in their thoughts and feelings, and validate their experiences.
2. Communicate openly and honestly: Create a safe space for open and honest communication. Encourage each other to express emotions and concerns without fear of judgment or criticism.

3. Seek to understand: Take the time to understand your partner's perspective, even if it differs from your own. Ask questions and engage in meaningful conversations to deepen your understanding of each other.

4. Show appreciation and gratitude: Express your appreciation for your partner's efforts and qualities. Acknowledge and celebrate their strengths, and let them know how much you value their presence in your life.

5. Practice forgiveness: Cultivate a forgiving mindset and let go of past hurts and resentments. Offer forgiveness to your partner and yourself, allowing room for growth and healing in your relationship.

6. Support each other's growth: Encourage and support each other's personal and emotional growth. Celebrate each other's achievements and provide a safe space for vulnerability and self-expression.

By actively cultivating empathy and compassion in your relationship, you create a strong foundation of love, understanding, and support. These qualities will not only enhance your connection but also help you navigate challenges and conflicts with grace and compassion. Remember, empathy and compassion are skills that can be developed and strengthened over time, so be patient with yourself and your partner as you embark on this journey together.

Remember, empathy and compassion are skills that can be developed and strengthened over time, so be patient with yourself and your partner as you embark on this journey together.

4

Chapter 4

4.Building a Strong Foundation

4.1 Establishing Trust and Honesty

Trust and honesty are the foundation upon which a strong and lasting relationship is built. Without these essential elements, a relationship is bound to crumble under the weight of doubt and insecurity. In this section, we will explore the importance of establishing trust and honesty in your relationship and provide you with practical strategies to cultivate these qualities.

4.1.1 The Importance of Trust

Trust is the cornerstone of any successful relationship. It is the belief that your partner is reliable, dependable, and has your best interests at heart. When trust is present, it creates a sense of safety and security, allowing both partners to be vulnerable and open with one another. Trust is not something that can be demanded or forced; it must be earned through consistent actions and behaviors.

Without trust, a relationship becomes a breeding ground for suspicion, jealousy, and resentment. Doubts and insecurities can erode the foundation of love and intimacy, leading to a breakdown in communication and emotional connection. Trust is the glue that holds a relationship together during challenging times and allows both partners to grow and evolve together.

4.1.2 Cultivating Honesty

Honesty is the bedrock of trust. It is the willingness to be open, transparent, and authentic in your communication with your partner. Honesty requires courage and vulnerability, as it involves sharing your thoughts, feelings, and experiences without fear of judgment or rejection.

Being honest with your partner means being true to yourself and your values. It means expressing your needs, desires, and boundaries in a clear and respectful manner. Honesty also involves taking responsibility for your actions and admitting when you make mistakes. By cultivating honesty in your relationship, you create an environment of mutual respect and understanding.

4.1.3 Building Trust Through Consistency

Trust is not built overnight; it is a gradual process that requires time, effort, and consistency. Here are some strategies to help you build trust in your relationship:

1. **Open Communication**: Foster open and honest communication with your partner. Encourage them to share their thoughts and feelings without fear of judgment or criticism. Create a safe space where both of you can express yourselves freely.
2. **Reliability**: Be reliable and consistent in your actions and commitments. Follow through on your promises and be there for your partner when they need you. Consistency builds trust and shows your partner that they can rely on you.
3. **Transparency**: Be transparent in your actions and intentions. Avoid

keeping secrets or hiding important information from your partner. Transparency builds trust and fosters a sense of security in the relationship.

4. **Accountability**: Take responsibility for your actions and admit when you make mistakes. Apologize sincerely and make amends when necessary. Being accountable shows your partner that you value their trust and are committed to the relationship.

5. **Boundaries**: Respect and honor each other's boundaries. Establish clear boundaries and communicate them openly. Respecting boundaries builds trust and creates a sense of safety within the relationship.

4.1.4 Rebuilding Trust After Betrayal

Trust can be fragile, and it may be broken due to betrayal or infidelity. Rebuilding trust after such a breach requires patience, understanding, and a commitment to healing. Here are some steps to help you rebuild trust:

1. **Open Communication**: Engage in open and honest communication about the betrayal. Allow your partner to express their feelings and concerns, and be willing to listen without becoming defensive.

2. **Accountability and Apology**: Take full responsibility for your actions and offer a sincere apology. Show genuine remorse and make a commitment to change your behavior.

3. **Transparency and Consistency**: Be transparent in your actions and intentions. Rebuild trust by consistently demonstrating trustworthy behavior over time. Follow through on your commitments and be reliable.

4. **Seek Professional Help**: Consider seeking the guidance of a couples therapist or relationship coach who specializes in trust-building. A professional can provide you with tools and strategies to navigate the healing process.

5. **Patience and Time**: Rebuilding trust takes time and patience. It is essential to allow your partner the space and time they need to heal. Be

understanding and supportive throughout the process.

Remember, rebuilding trust is a joint effort. Both partners must be committed to the process and willing to work through the challenges that arise. With time, effort, and a genuine desire to rebuild, trust can be restored, and the relationship can grow stronger than ever before.

In the next section, we will explore the importance of setting boundaries and respecting each other's autonomy in a relationship.

4.2 Setting Boundaries and Respecting Each Other's Autonomy

Setting boundaries and respecting each other's autonomy is a crucial aspect of building a strong foundation in any relationship. Boundaries serve as guidelines that define what is acceptable and unacceptable behavior within the relationship, while respecting each other's autonomy ensures that both partners have the freedom to be themselves and pursue their individual interests and goals. In this section, we will explore the importance of setting boundaries, how to establish them effectively, and the significance of respecting each other's autonomy.

4.2.1 Understanding the Importance of Boundaries

Boundaries are essential in relationships because they create a sense of safety, trust, and respect. They help establish clear expectations and prevent misunderstandings or conflicts from arising. When both partners understand and respect each other's boundaries, it fosters a healthy and balanced dynamic where both individuals feel valued and heard.

Boundaries also play a crucial role in maintaining individual identities within a relationship. It is important for each partner to have their own space, interests, and goals outside of the relationship. By setting boundaries, individuals can ensure that their personal needs are met and that they have the freedom to pursue their passions and maintain a sense of self.

4.2.2 Establishing Boundaries Effectively

Establishing boundaries requires open and honest communication between partners. It is important to have a conversation about each other's needs, desires, and limits. Here are some steps to help you establish boundaries effectively:

1. Self-reflection: Take the time to reflect on your own needs, values, and limits. Understand what is important to you and what you are comfortable with in a relationship.

2. Communicate openly: Express your boundaries to your partner in a clear and respectful manner. Use "I" statements to avoid sounding accusatory and focus on your own feelings and needs.

3. Active listening: Give your partner the space to express their boundaries as well. Listen attentively and validate their feelings and needs. Remember, boundaries are a two-way street, and both partners should have the opportunity to express themselves.

4. Negotiation and compromise: In some cases, boundaries may need to be negotiated to find a middle ground that works for both partners. Be open to compromise and find solutions that respect both individuals' needs.

5. Consistency and reinforcement: Once boundaries are established, it is important to consistently uphold them. Reinforce the importance of boundaries by respecting them and encouraging your partner to do the same.

4.2.3 Respecting Each Other's Autonomy

Respecting each other's autonomy means acknowledging and supporting each other's individuality, independence, and personal choices. It involves recognizing that both partners have their own unique identities, interests, and goals outside of the relationship. Here are some key aspects of respecting each other's autonomy:

1. Encouraging personal growth: Support your partner's personal growth and encourage them to pursue their passions and interests. Celebrate their achievements and provide a safe space for them to explore their individuality.

2. Trust and independence: Trust is the foundation of respecting each other's autonomy. Allow your partner the freedom to make their own decisions and respect their choices, even if they differ from your own.

3. Open communication: Maintain open lines of communication and encourage your partner to express their thoughts, feelings, and desires. Create a safe and non-judgmental environment where both partners can freely share their perspectives.

4. Avoiding control and possessiveness: Recognize that your partner is not an extension of yourself. Avoid controlling behaviors or possessiveness that may limit their autonomy. Trust that both partners can maintain their individuality while still being committed to the relationship.

Respecting each other's autonomy does not mean neglecting the relationship or disregarding each other's needs. It means finding a balance between individuality and togetherness, where both partners feel supported and valued.

Conclusion

Setting boundaries and respecting each other's autonomy are vital components of a healthy and fulfilling relationship. By establishing clear boundaries and honoring each other's individuality, couples can create a strong foundation built on trust, respect, and open communication. Remember, relationships thrive when both partners feel safe, heard, and free to be themselves.

4.3 Managing Conflict and Resolving Differences

Conflict is an inevitable part of any relationship. No matter how compatible you and your partner may be, disagreements and differences of opinion are bound to arise. However, it is how you manage and resolve these conflicts that can make or break the strength of your relationship. In this section, we will explore effective strategies for managing conflict and resolving differences in a healthy and constructive manner.

4.3.1 Understanding the Nature of Conflict

Conflict arises when two individuals have differing needs, desires, or perspectives. It can manifest in various forms, such as disagreements, arguments, or even silent tension. It is important to recognize that conflict is not inherently negative or destructive. In fact, conflict can be an opportunity for growth, understanding, and deeper connection if approached with the right mindset and skills.

4.3.2 Cultivating Effective Communication

Effective communication is the foundation for managing conflict and resolving differences. It involves actively listening to your partner, expressing your thoughts and feelings clearly and respectfully, and seeking to understand their perspective. When conflicts arise, it is crucial to create a safe and non-judgmental space for open and honest dialogue.

One key aspect of effective communication is active listening. This means giving your partner your full attention, maintaining eye contact, and genuinely seeking to understand their point of view. It also involves reflecting back what you have heard to ensure that you have understood correctly. Active listening helps to foster empathy and promotes a sense of validation and understanding between partners.

4.3.3 Finding Common Ground

Resolving conflicts often requires finding common ground and seeking mutually beneficial solutions. This involves identifying shared goals and interests and working together to find compromises that meet both partners' needs. It is important to approach conflict resolution with a mindset of collaboration rather than competition.

During the process of finding common ground, it is essential to remain open-minded and flexible. This means being willing to consider alternative perspectives and being open to adjusting your own views if necessary. Remember, the goal is not to "win" the argument but to find a resolution that strengthens the relationship and honors the needs and values of both partners.

4.3.4 Managing Emotions

Conflict can evoke strong emotions, such as anger, frustration, or sadness. It is crucial to manage these emotions effectively during the conflict resolution process. This involves practicing emotional regulation techniques, such as deep breathing, taking breaks when needed, and using "I" statements to express your feelings without blaming or attacking your partner.

It is also important to cultivate empathy and compassion towards your partner's emotions. Recognize that they may be experiencing their own set of emotions and validate their feelings, even if you disagree with their perspective. By acknowledging and validating each other's emotions, you create a safe space for open and honest communication.

4.3.5 Seeking Professional Help

In some cases, conflicts may be deeply rooted or complex, requiring the assistance of a trained professional. Seeking couples therapy or relationship counseling can provide valuable guidance and support in navigating challenging conflicts. A skilled therapist can help you and your partner develop effective communication strategies, explore underlying issues, and facilitate the resolution of conflicts in a neutral and unbiased manner.

Remember, conflict is a natural part of any relationship, and it is how you manage and resolve it that determines the strength and longevity of your connection. By cultivating effective communication skills, seeking common ground, managing emotions, and being open to professional help when needed, you can navigate conflicts in a healthy and constructive way. Conflict resolution is an opportunity for growth, understanding, and deepening your bond with your partner. Embrace it as a chance to strengthen your relationship and create a lasting love.

4.4 Nurturing Intimacy and Connection

Intimacy and connection are the lifeblood of a thriving relationship. They are the threads that weave two individuals together, creating a bond that withstands the tests of time. Nurturing intimacy and connection requires effort, intention, and a deep understanding of each other's needs and desires. In this section, we will explore the various ways in which you can cultivate and strengthen the intimacy and connection in your relationship.

4.4.1 Creating Emotional Intimacy

Emotional intimacy forms the foundation of a strong and lasting relationship. It is the ability to be vulnerable, open, and authentic with your partner, allowing them to see and understand the depths of your emotions. To create emotional intimacy, it is crucial to cultivate a safe and non-judgmental space where both partners feel comfortable expressing their true selves.

One way to foster emotional intimacy is through active listening and validation. This involves giving your partner your full attention, truly hearing their words, and acknowledging their feelings. By validating their experiences and emotions, you show them that you value and respect their perspective. This deepens the emotional connection between you and builds trust.

Another important aspect of emotional intimacy is sharing your needs and desires with your partner. By expressing your wants and needs, you allow your partner to understand you on a deeper level and create opportunities for them to meet those needs. This open and honest communication fosters a sense of emotional closeness and strengthens the bond between you.

4.4.2 Cultivating Physical Intimacy

Physical intimacy is an essential component of a romantic relationship. It encompasses not only sexual connection but also non-sexual touch, affection, and closeness. Cultivating physical intimacy requires creating a safe and comfortable space where both partners feel desired, respected, and cherished.

Enhancing sexual connection involves open and honest communication about desires, boundaries, and preferences. By exploring each other's fantasies and desires, you can create a space where both partners feel comfortable expressing their sexual needs. This mutual exploration can deepen the physical connection and bring a sense of excitement and fulfillment to the relationship.

Non-sexual touch and affection are equally important in nurturing physical intimacy. Simple acts of holding hands, hugging, cuddling, or giving each other massages can create a sense of closeness and reinforce the bond between partners. These acts of physical affection communicate love, care, and support, fostering a deeper connection.

4.4.3 Building Rituals of Connection

Rituals of connection are intentional practices that couples engage in to strengthen their bond and create a sense of shared meaning. These rituals can be as simple as having a weekly date night, cooking together, or taking walks in nature. The key is to create regular opportunities for quality time and connection.

By establishing rituals of connection, you create a sense of predictability and stability in your relationship. These rituals serve as anchors that remind you of your commitment to each other and provide a space for deepening your emotional and physical intimacy. They also offer an opportunity to explore new experiences together, fostering growth and shared memories.

4.4.4 Practicing Gratitude and Appreciation

Gratitude and appreciation are powerful tools for nurturing intimacy and connection. Taking the time to acknowledge and express gratitude for your partner's presence, efforts, and qualities can create a positive and loving atmosphere in your relationship. It shows your partner that you see and value their contributions, fostering a sense of mutual appreciation.

Practicing gratitude and appreciation can be as simple as saying "thank you" for the little things your partner does or writing them a heartfelt note expressing your love and gratitude. It is important to cultivate a habit of noticing and acknowledging the positive aspects of your relationship, even during challenging times. This practice strengthens the bond between you and reinforces the foundation of love and connection.

In conclusion, nurturing intimacy and connection is a continuous process that requires effort, intention, and a deep understanding of each other's needs. By creating emotional intimacy, cultivating physical intimacy, building rituals of connection, and practicing gratitude and appreciation, you can strengthen the bond in your relationship and create a lasting love. Remember, the journey towards a fulfilling and connected relationship is a lifelong one, and the rewards are immeasurable.

5

Chapter 5

5.Effective Communication

5.1 Active Listening and Validation

Effective communication is the cornerstone of any successful relationship. It is through communication that we express our needs, desires, and emotions, and it is through active listening and validation that we create a safe and supportive space for our partners to do the same. In this section, we will explore the importance of active listening and validation in building strong and lasting connections with our partners.

5.1.1 The Power of Active Listening

Active listening is a skill that allows us to fully engage with our partners and understand their perspectives, thoughts, and feelings. It involves giving our full attention, both verbally and non-verbally, to the person speaking, without interrupting or judging. By actively listening, we show our partners that we value and respect their experiences, fostering a sense of trust and emotional intimacy.

To practice active listening, start by creating a space free from distractions.

Put away your phone, turn off the TV, and make eye contact with your partner. Focus on what they are saying, rather than formulating your response. Use non-verbal cues, such as nodding or maintaining an open posture, to show that you are engaged in the conversation. Reflect back on what your partner has said, paraphrasing their words to ensure understanding. This not only demonstrates that you are actively listening, but also allows for clarification and deeper connection.

5.1.2 The Importance of Validation

Validation is the act of acknowledging and accepting our partner's thoughts, feelings, and experiences as valid and understandable. It is a powerful tool in building emotional connection and fostering a sense of security within the relationship. When we validate our partner, we communicate that their emotions and experiences matter to us, and that we are there to support and understand them.

Validation involves both verbal and non-verbal cues. Verbal validation can be as simple as saying, "I understand how you feel," or "That must have been really difficult for you." It is important to avoid dismissing or minimizing our partner's emotions, as this can lead to feelings of invalidation and disconnection. Non-verbal validation can be expressed through physical touch, such as a comforting hug or holding hands, or through facial expressions that convey empathy and understanding.

5.1.3 The Benefits of Active Listening and Validation

Active listening and validation have numerous benefits for both individuals and the relationship as a whole. When we actively listen to our partners and validate their experiences, we create a safe and supportive environment where open and honest communication can thrive. This leads to increased emotional intimacy, trust, and connection.

By actively listening and validating our partners, we also demonstrate respect and empathy, which are essential components of a healthy and loving relationship. When our partners feel heard and understood, they are more likely to reciprocate these behaviors, creating a positive cycle of communication and understanding.

Furthermore, active listening and validation can help prevent and resolve conflicts. When we truly listen to our partners and validate their emotions, we are better equipped to find mutually satisfactory solutions and compromise. This reduces the likelihood of misunderstandings and resentment, fostering a more harmonious and fulfilling relationship.

5.1.4 Practicing Active Listening and Validation

Like any skill, active listening and validation require practice and intentionality. Here are some practical tips to incorporate these skills into your daily interactions with your partner:

1. Create dedicated time for meaningful conversations: Set aside regular time to have deep and meaningful conversations with your partner. This can be during a designated "check-in" time or during activities such as walks or shared meals.
2. Be present and attentive: Eliminate distractions and give your partner your undivided attention. Put away electronic devices and focus on the person in front of you.
3. Use open-ended questions: Encourage your partner to share their thoughts and feelings by asking open-ended questions. This allows for more in-depth conversations and promotes active listening.
4. Reflect and paraphrase: After your partner has shared their thoughts or feelings, reflect back on what they have said to ensure understanding. Paraphrase their words and ask for clarification if needed.
5. Validate their emotions: Acknowledge and accept your partner's emotions as valid and understandable. Avoid dismissing or minimizing their feelings, and instead, offer empathy and support.
6. Practice empathy: Put yourself in your partner's shoes and try to understand their perspective. This will help you respond with compassion

and validation.

Remember, active listening and validation are ongoing practices that require effort and commitment. By incorporating these skills into your daily interactions, you can create a strong foundation of communication and understanding in your relationship.

5.2 Expressing Needs and Desires

In any relationship, it is essential to be able to express your needs and desires effectively. Open and honest communication is the foundation for building a strong and lasting connection with your partner. When you can clearly articulate what you want and need, it allows your partner to understand you better and work towards meeting those needs. In this section, we will explore the importance of expressing your needs and desires and provide you with practical strategies to do so in a healthy and constructive manner.

5.2.1 Understanding the Importance of Expressing Needs and Desires

Expressing your needs and desires is crucial for several reasons. Firstly, it allows you to establish boundaries and communicate what is important to you in the relationship. By clearly expressing your needs, you create an opportunity for your partner to understand and support you. This open communication fosters trust and intimacy, as your partner learns more about your inner world and what makes you feel loved and fulfilled.

Secondly, expressing your needs and desires helps prevent resentment and frustration from building up over time. When you suppress your needs, it can lead to feelings of neglect or being taken for granted. By openly communicating your desires, you give your partner the chance to address them and work towards a mutually satisfying solution. This proactive approach promotes a healthier and more balanced dynamic within the relationship.

Lastly, expressing your needs and desires promotes personal growth and self-awareness. It allows you to reflect on your own wants and needs, helping you gain a deeper understanding of yourself. By sharing these insights with your partner, you invite them to support you in your journey of self-discovery and growth. This mutual support and understanding can strengthen the bond between you and create a sense of shared purpose within the relationship.

5.2.2 Strategies for Expressing Needs and Desires

1. Self-reflection: Before expressing your needs and desires to your partner, take some time for self-reflection. Clarify what you truly want and need in the relationship. Consider your values, priorities, and long-term goals. This self-awareness will help you communicate your needs more effectively and avoid any confusion or misunderstandings.

2. Choose the right time and place: Timing is crucial when it comes to expressing your needs and desires. Find a calm and comfortable environment where both you and your partner can have an open and uninterrupted conversation. Avoid discussing sensitive topics when either of you is tired, stressed, or distracted. Creating a safe space for communication sets the stage for a productive and constructive dialogue.

3. Use "I" statements: When expressing your needs and desires, use "I" statements instead of "you" statements. This approach focuses on your own feelings and experiences, rather than placing blame or making accusations. For example, instead of saying, "You never spend enough time with me," try saying, "I feel lonely when we don't have quality time together." This shift in language encourages empathy and understanding from your partner's perspective.

4. Be specific and clear: Clearly articulate your needs and desires to avoid any ambiguity. Vague or general statements can lead to misunderstandings and frustration. Instead, provide specific examples and details to help your partner understand exactly what you are asking for. For instance, instead of saying, "I want more affection," you could say, "I would love it if we could cuddle for at least 10 minutes every evening before bed."

5. Practice active listening: Effective communication is a two-way street. When expressing your needs and desires, encourage your partner to share their thoughts and feelings as well. Practice active listening by giving your full attention, maintaining eye contact, and validating their perspective. This creates a safe and supportive environment for open dialogue and fosters mutual understanding.

6. Seek compromise and collaboration: Remember that relationships require compromise and collaboration. Be open to finding solutions that meet both your needs and your partner's needs. Approach the conversation with a mindset of finding a win-win outcome rather than trying to "win" the argument. By working together, you can create a relationship that honors both individuals' desires and fosters a sense of shared growth and fulfillment.

Conclusion

Expressing your needs and desires is an essential aspect of building a healthy and fulfilling relationship. By openly communicating what you want and need, you create an opportunity for your partner to understand and support you. Remember to approach these conversations with empathy, clarity, and a willingness to collaborate. When both partners can express their needs and desires effectively, it strengthens the foundation of the relationship and paves the way for lasting love and happiness.

5.3 Nonviolent Communication Techniques

In any relationship, communication plays a vital role in fostering understanding, connection, and resolving conflicts. However, traditional communication methods often fall short in creating a safe and compassionate space for both partners to express their needs and desires. This is where nonviolent communication techniques come into play.

Nonviolent communication, also known as compassionate communication or NVC, is a powerful tool that allows individuals to express themselves authentically while promoting empathy and understanding in their interactions. Developed by psychologist Marshall Rosenberg, NVC focuses on fostering connection, resolving conflicts, and building trust through compassionate and nonjudgmental communication.

5.3.1 The Four Components of Nonviolent Communication

Nonviolent communication consists of four key components that guide individuals in expressing themselves effectively and empathetically:

1. **Observation**: The first step in nonviolent communication is to observe and describe the situation or behavior without judgment or evaluation. By focusing on the facts rather than interpretations, individuals can communicate their observations in a neutral and non-threatening manner.
2. **Feeling**: After observing the situation, it is essential to identify and express the emotions that arise. Nonviolent communication encourages individuals to connect with their feelings and express them honestly, allowing their partners to understand their emotional state.
3. **Need**: Once the feelings are acknowledged, it is crucial to identify the underlying needs or values that are driving those emotions. Nonviolent communication emphasizes the importance of recognizing and expressing these needs, as they are often at the core of conflicts and misunderstandings.
4. **Request**: The final component of nonviolent communication involves making clear and specific requests that address the identified needs. By formulating requests rather than demands, individuals create an opportunity for collaboration and mutual understanding, fostering a sense of partnership in resolving conflicts.

5.3.2 Empathy and Active Listening

Empathy is a fundamental aspect of nonviolent communication. It involves actively listening to your partner's perspective, understanding their feelings and needs, and responding with compassion and understanding. When practicing empathy, it is essential to suspend judgment, truly listen, and validate your partner's experience.

Active listening is a crucial skill in nonviolent communication. It involves giving your full attention to your partner, maintaining eye contact, and providing verbal and nonverbal cues that show you are engaged in the conversation. By actively listening, you create a safe space for your partner to express themselves fully, fostering trust and connection in the relationship.

5.3.3 Expressing Yourself with Honesty and Compassion

Nonviolent communication encourages individuals to express themselves honestly while maintaining compassion and empathy for their partner. It is essential to communicate your needs, desires, and boundaries clearly and assertively, without resorting to blame or criticism.

When expressing yourself, it is crucial to use "I" statements to take ownership of your feelings and experiences. This approach avoids placing blame on your partner and instead focuses on your own perspective. For example, instead of saying, "You never listen to me," you can say, "I feel unheard when I don't feel listened to."

Additionally, nonviolent communication emphasizes the importance of using neutral and nonjudgmental language. By avoiding labels and evaluations, you create a space where both partners can express themselves without fear of judgment or criticism.

5.3.4 Resolving Conflicts Peacefully

Conflicts are a natural part of any relationship, but how they are handled can make a significant difference in the overall health and longevity of the partnership. Nonviolent communication provides effective strategies for resolving conflicts peacefully and fostering understanding.

One technique commonly used in nonviolent communication is the "Giraffe and Jackal" metaphor. The giraffe represents the compassionate and empathetic approach, while the jackal symbolizes the critical and judgmental mindset. By consciously choosing the giraffe approach, individuals can navigate conflicts with empathy, understanding, and a focus on finding mutually beneficial solutions.

Another valuable technique in conflict resolution is the practice of reflective listening. This involves paraphrasing and summarizing your partner's perspective to ensure that you have understood their feelings and needs accurately. Reflective listening not only demonstrates your commitment to understanding but also helps to clarify any misunderstandings and promotes a sense of validation.

5.3.5 Cultivating Mindfulness in Communication

Mindfulness is a powerful tool in nonviolent communication. By cultivating present-moment awareness, individuals can become more attuned to their own emotions, thoughts, and reactions during communication. This self-awareness allows for more intentional and conscious communication, reducing the likelihood of reactive and harmful responses.

Practicing mindfulness in communication involves being fully present in the conversation, listening without judgment, and responding with intention and compassion. By staying mindful, individuals can avoid falling into patterns of defensiveness, criticism, or blame, creating a space for open and honest dialogue.

In conclusion, nonviolent communication techniques provide a framework for fostering understanding, empathy, and connection in relationships. By incorporating these techniques into your communication style, you can create a safe and compassionate space for both partners to express their needs, resolve conflicts peacefully, and cultivate a lasting and fulfilling love.

5.4 Conflict Resolution Strategies

Conflict is an inevitable part of any relationship. No matter how compatible you and your partner may be, disagreements and misunderstandings are bound to arise. The key to maintaining a healthy and lasting relationship lies in how you handle these conflicts. In this section, we will explore effective conflict resolution strategies that can help you navigate through disagreements and strengthen your bond with your partner.

5.4.1 Active Listening and Empathy

One of the most important skills in conflict resolution is active listening. When conflicts arise, it is crucial to give your partner your full attention and truly listen to what they have to say. Active listening involves not only hearing their words but also understanding their emotions and perspective. Show empathy by putting yourself in their shoes and trying to see the situation from their point of view. This will help create a safe and supportive environment for open communication.

5.4.2 Expressing Needs and Desires

In any conflict, it is essential to express your needs and desires clearly and assertively. Avoid using accusatory language or blaming your partner. Instead, use "I" statements to express how you feel and what you need from the situation. For example, instead of saying, "You never listen to me," try saying, "I feel unheard when we have disagreements, and I need us to find a way to communicate better." By expressing your needs in a non-confrontational manner, you are more likely to be heard and understood by your partner.

5.4.3 Finding Common Ground and Compromise

Conflict resolution is not about winning or losing; it is about finding a solution that works for both partners. Look for areas of common ground and shared goals that you can build upon. Focus on finding a compromise that addresses both of your needs and allows for mutual growth and understanding. Remember that compromise does not mean sacrificing your values or needs; it means finding a middle ground that respects both individuals in the relationship.

5.4.4 Taking a Time-Out

Sometimes, conflicts can become heated and emotions can run high. In such situations, it is important to recognize when it is necessary to take a time-out. If you feel overwhelmed or unable to communicate effectively, suggest taking a break from the discussion. Use this time to calm down, reflect on your feelings, and gather your thoughts. Agree on a specific time to reconvene and continue the conversation when both partners are in a better emotional state.

5.4.5 Seeking Mediation or Professional Help

In some cases, conflicts may persist despite your best efforts to resolve them. If you find yourselves stuck in a cycle of unresolved issues, it may be beneficial to seek outside help. Consider seeking mediation from a neutral third party, such as a therapist or counselor, who can provide guidance and facilitate productive communication. Professional help can offer new perspectives and strategies for resolving conflicts and strengthening your relationship.

5.4.6 Practicing Forgiveness and Letting Go

Conflict resolution also involves the ability to forgive and let go of past grievances. Holding onto grudges and resentments can hinder the progress of conflict resolution and prevent healing within the relationship. Practice forgiveness by acknowledging your partner's efforts to resolve conflicts and letting go of any lingering negative emotions. Remember that forgiveness does not mean forgetting or condoning hurtful behavior, but rather choosing to move forward and rebuild trust.

5.4.7 Learning from Conflict

Conflict can be an opportunity for growth and learning within a relationship. Instead of viewing conflicts as negative experiences, approach them as opportunities to gain a deeper understanding of yourself and your partner. Reflect on the underlying causes of the conflict and identify any patterns or triggers that may contribute to recurring issues. Use these insights to develop strategies for preventing future conflicts and fostering a more harmonious relationship.

5.4.8 Cultivating Patience and Resilience

Conflict resolution takes time and patience. It is important to remember that not all conflicts can be resolved immediately or completely. Cultivate patience and resilience as you work through conflicts with your partner. Understand that it is normal to encounter setbacks and challenges along the way. Stay committed to the process of resolving conflicts and nurturing your relationship, even when it feels difficult or overwhelming.

By implementing these conflict resolution strategies, you can create a foundation of open communication, understanding, and mutual respect within your relationship. Remember that conflicts are not a sign of failure but an opportunity for growth and deeper connection. Embrace the challenges that arise and approach them with a willingness to learn and evolve together.

With the right skills and mindset, you can navigate conflicts successfully and build a lasting love.

6

Chapter 6

6.Maintaining Emotional and Sexual Intimacy

6.1 Understanding Emotional Intimacy

Emotional intimacy is a fundamental aspect of any healthy and lasting relationship. It is the deep connection and bond that is formed between two individuals, allowing them to feel safe, understood, and supported by one another. In this section, we will explore the importance of emotional intimacy, how it can be nurtured and maintained, and its role in creating a strong foundation for love.

The Power of Emotional Intimacy

Emotional intimacy goes beyond physical attraction or shared interests. It involves a deep level of vulnerability and openness, where individuals feel comfortable expressing their true selves without fear of judgment or rejection. When emotional intimacy is present in a relationship, it creates a safe space for both partners to be authentic and genuine, fostering a sense of trust and security.

One of the key benefits of emotional intimacy is the ability to truly understand and empathize with your partner. It allows you to connect on a deeper level, to share your hopes, dreams, fears, and insecurities, and to be fully present for one another. This level of connection can enhance the overall quality of the relationship, leading to greater satisfaction and fulfillment.

Cultivating Emotional Intimacy

Building emotional intimacy requires effort and intentionality from both partners. It involves creating an environment where open and honest communication is encouraged, and where both individuals feel safe to express their emotions and needs. Here are some strategies to cultivate emotional intimacy in your relationship:

6.1.1 Active Listening and Empathy

Active listening is a crucial skill in fostering emotional intimacy. It involves giving your partner your full attention, being present in the moment, and truly hearing what they are saying. Practice empathy by putting yourself in their shoes and trying to understand their perspective. Validate their feelings and experiences, even if you may not fully agree or relate to them.

6.1.2 Sharing Vulnerabilities

To deepen emotional intimacy, it is important to share your vulnerabilities with your partner. This means being open and honest about your fears, insecurities, and past experiences that have shaped you. By sharing these aspects of yourself, you allow your partner to see the real you and create a space for them to do the same.

6.1.3 Building Trust and Safety

Trust is the foundation of emotional intimacy. It is essential to create a safe and non-judgmental environment where both partners feel comfortable being vulnerable. Honesty, reliability, and consistency are key elements in building trust. By demonstrating trustworthiness and respecting each other's boundaries, you can foster a sense of safety and security within the relationship.

6.1.4 Emotional Support and Validation

Providing emotional support and validation is crucial in nurturing emotional intimacy. Show empathy and understanding when your partner is going through a difficult time. Validate their emotions and experiences, letting them know that their feelings are heard and acknowledged. Offer comfort and reassurance, and be a source of strength and encouragement for one another.

The Role of Emotional Intimacy in Sexual Connection

Emotional intimacy and sexual connection are deeply intertwined. When emotional intimacy is present in a relationship, it can enhance the level of trust and vulnerability during intimate moments. Emotional closeness allows partners to feel safe and secure, creating an environment where they can freely express their desires and needs.

Intimacy in the bedroom is not solely about physical pleasure; it is about the emotional connection and mutual understanding between partners. Emotional intimacy can deepen the level of passion and desire, as partners feel more connected on a holistic level. By nurturing emotional intimacy, you can enhance the overall quality of your sexual relationship.

Sustaining Emotional Intimacy in the Long Term

Maintaining emotional intimacy requires ongoing effort and commitment. As relationships evolve and face various challenges, it is important to prioritize emotional connection. Here are some strategies to sustain emotional intimacy in the long term:

6.1.5 Regular Check-Ins

Schedule regular check-ins with your partner to discuss your emotional needs, desires, and concerns. This dedicated time allows you to connect on a deeper level and address any issues that may arise. Use this opportunity to express gratitude, share your feelings, and reaffirm your commitment to one another.

6.1.6 Quality Time and Shared Experiences

Carve out quality time for each other, free from distractions, to nurture emotional intimacy. Engage in activities that you both enjoy and create shared experiences that strengthen your bond. Whether it's going on a date night, taking a walk together, or simply cuddling on the couch, prioritize time to connect and deepen your emotional connection.

6.1.7 Continual Growth and Learning

Emotional intimacy thrives when both partners are committed to personal growth and learning. Encourage each other to pursue individual interests, engage in self-reflection, and seek personal development. By continually growing as individuals, you bring new experiences and perspectives into the relationship, fostering emotional depth and connection.

6.1.8 Open and Honest Communication

Maintaining open and honest communication is vital in sustaining emotional intimacy. Regularly check in with each other about your emotional needs, desires, and concerns. Be willing to listen and understand your partner's perspective, and be open to constructive feedback. By fostering a culture of open communication, you create a safe space for emotional intimacy to flourish.

In conclusion, emotional intimacy is a cornerstone of a healthy and lasting relationship, more so than sexual intimacy. It requires effort, vulnerability, and a commitment to ongoing growth and connection. By cultivating emotional intimacy, you create a strong foundation for love, trust, and mutual understanding. Remember, emotional intimacy is a journey, and it requires continual nurturing and attention to thrive.

6.2 Sustaining Intimacy in Long-Term Relationships

Sustaining intimacy in long-term relationships is a crucial aspect of maintaining a happy and fulfilling partnership. As the initial excitement and novelty of a relationship begin to fade, it is essential to cultivate and nurture the emotional and physical connection between partners. This chapter will explore various strategies and techniques to help you sustain intimacy in your long-term relationship.

6.2.1 Prioritizing Emotional Connection

Emotional intimacy forms the foundation of a strong and lasting relationship. It involves deepening the bond between partners by fostering trust, vulnerability, and open communication. To sustain emotional intimacy, it is important to prioritize quality time together and engage in activities that promote emotional connection.

One effective way to enhance emotional intimacy is through regular and meaningful conversations. Set aside dedicated time to talk about your feelings, dreams, and aspirations. Share your fears, hopes, and challenges with each other, creating a safe space for vulnerability and understanding. Active listening and empathy play a crucial role in fostering emotional intimacy, allowing both partners to feel heard and validated.

6.2.2 Nurturing Physical Intimacy

Physical intimacy is an integral part of a romantic relationship and plays a significant role in sustaining long-term intimacy. It encompasses not only sexual intimacy but also non-sexual physical affection, such as cuddling, holding hands, and hugging. Nurturing physical intimacy requires open communication, exploration, and a willingness to adapt to each other's changing needs and desires.

To sustain physical intimacy, it is important to prioritize quality time for physical connection. This can involve setting aside regular date nights, engaging in activities that promote physical closeness, and expressing affection through touch and gestures. Remember that physical intimacy is not solely about sexual activity but also about creating a sense of closeness and connection.

6.2.3 Cultivating Novelty and Adventure

One common challenge in long-term relationships is the potential for monotony and routine. To sustain intimacy, it is important to introduce novelty and adventure into your relationship. Engaging in new experiences together can reignite the spark and create shared memories that deepen your bond.

Consider exploring new hobbies or activities as a couple, planning surprise dates or getaways, or even trying new things in the bedroom. By stepping outside of your comfort zones and embracing new experiences, you can infuse excitement and freshness into your relationship.

6.2.4 Practicing Gratitude and Appreciation

Expressing gratitude and appreciation for your partner is a powerful way to sustain intimacy in a long-term relationship. Taking the time to acknowledge and celebrate each other's strengths, efforts, and contributions can foster a sense of love and connection.

Make it a habit to regularly express gratitude for the little things your partner does, whether it's preparing a meal, offering emotional support, or simply being there for you. Additionally, celebrate milestones and anniversaries as opportunities to reflect on your journey together and express gratitude for the growth and love you have shared.

6.2.5 Prioritizing Self-Care and Personal Growth

Sustaining intimacy in a long-term relationship requires individuals to prioritize their own well-being and personal growth. Taking care of yourself physically, emotionally, and mentally allows you to show up fully in your relationship and maintain a healthy balance between independence and togetherness.

Engage in activities that bring you joy and fulfillment outside of your relationship. Pursue your passions, invest in self-reflection and personal growth, and prioritize self-care. By nurturing your own well-being, you can bring a sense of vitality and authenticity to your relationship, enhancing the overall intimacy and connection.

6.2.6 Seeking Professional Support

Sometimes, sustaining intimacy in a long-term relationship can be challenging, and it may be beneficial to seek professional support. Relationship therapists or counselors can provide guidance, tools, and strategies to navigate any obstacles or difficulties you may encounter.

Don't hesitate to reach out for help if you feel stuck or overwhelmed. Seeking professional support is a proactive step towards sustaining intimacy and ensuring the long-term success of your relationship.

Remember, sustaining intimacy in a long-term relationship requires effort, commitment, and continuous growth. By prioritizing emotional connection, nurturing physical intimacy, cultivating novelty and adventure, practicing gratitude and appreciation, prioritizing self-care and personal growth, and seeking professional support when needed, you can create a lasting and fulfilling love that stands the test of time.

7

Chapter 7

7.Navigating Challenges and Transitions

7.1 Managing Stress and External Pressures

In any relationship, stress and external pressures are inevitable. Life is full of challenges, and it's important to learn how to navigate these obstacles together as a couple. Managing stress and external pressures is a crucial skill that can help strengthen your bond and ensure the longevity of your relationship.

Understanding the Impact of Stress on Relationships

Stress can have a significant impact on relationships. It can lead to increased tension, decreased communication, and a lack of emotional connection. When stressors such as work pressures, financial difficulties, or family issues arise, it's essential to recognize their potential impact on your relationship.

Stress can manifest in various ways, including irritability, mood swings, and a lack of patience. It's important to remember that these reactions are often a result of external pressures and not a reflection of your love for each other. By understanding the impact of stress on your relationship, you can approach these challenges with empathy and compassion.

Effective Communication during Stressful Times

During times of stress, effective communication becomes even more critical. It's essential to create a safe and supportive space where both partners can express their feelings and concerns openly. Active listening and validation are key components of effective communication during stressful times.

Active listening involves giving your full attention to your partner, maintaining eye contact, and acknowledging their emotions. It's important to validate their feelings and let them know that you understand and empathize with their experience. By practicing active listening and validation, you can foster a sense of emotional support and strengthen your connection.

Seeking Support from Each Other

When facing external pressures, it's crucial to lean on each other for support. Remember that you are a team, and together you can overcome any challenge. By openly discussing your concerns and seeking comfort from each other, you can create a sense of unity and resilience.

Supporting each other during stressful times involves being present, offering encouragement, and providing a listening ear. It's important to validate each other's experiences and emotions, even if you may not fully understand or agree with them. By offering support and understanding, you can create a safe space for vulnerability and strengthen your bond.

Prioritizing Self-Care

Managing stress and external pressures also requires prioritizing self-care. It's essential to take care of your own well-being so that you can show up as your best self in the relationship. This includes engaging in activities that bring you joy, practicing self-compassion, and setting boundaries when needed.

Self-care can take many forms, such as engaging in hobbies, practicing mindfulness or meditation, exercising regularly, and maintaining a healthy work-life balance. By prioritizing self-care, you can recharge and replenish your energy, allowing you to better navigate the challenges that come your way.

Seeking Professional Help

In some cases, managing stress and external pressures may require seeking professional help. If you find that the challenges you're facing are overwhelming and impacting your relationship, it's important to consider couples therapy or counseling. A trained professional can provide guidance, tools, and strategies to help you navigate these challenges effectively.

Therapy can offer a safe and neutral space for both partners to express their concerns, explore underlying issues, and develop healthy coping mechanisms. It can also provide a fresh perspective and help you gain a deeper understanding of each other's needs and perspectives.

Embracing Flexibility and Adaptability

Lastly, managing stress and external pressures requires embracing flexibility and adaptability. Life is unpredictable, and circumstances may change unexpectedly. By being open to adapting your plans and expectations, you can navigate these challenges with greater ease.

Flexibility involves being willing to compromise, finding creative solutions, and adjusting your approach when necessary. It's important to remember that relationships are dynamic and require ongoing effort and adaptation. By embracing flexibility, you can navigate the ups and downs of life together and emerge stronger as a couple.

Remember, managing stress and external pressures is an ongoing process. It requires continuous effort, effective communication, and a commitment to supporting each other through life's challenges. By developing these skills, you can create a resilient and thriving relationship that can withstand the tests of time.

7.2 Dealing with Life Changes and Transitions

Life is full of changes and transitions, and navigating them can be challenging for any relationship. Whether it's a new job, a move to a different city, the birth of a child, or the loss of a loved one, these life changes can put a strain on even the strongest of partnerships. In this section, we will explore strategies and techniques to help you and your partner effectively deal with life changes and transitions, ensuring that your relationship remains strong and resilient.

7.2.1 Embracing Change Together

Change is inevitable, and it is important to approach it as a team. When faced with a significant life change, it is crucial to communicate openly and honestly with your partner. Share your fears, concerns, and hopes for the future. By expressing your emotions and thoughts, you can create a safe space for both of you to process the changes and find ways to support each other.

7.2.2 Adapting to New Roles and Responsibilities

Life changes often come with new roles and responsibilities. It is essential to have open discussions about how these changes will impact your daily lives and the division of labor within your relationship. By openly discussing and negotiating these new roles, you can ensure that both partners feel valued and supported.

7.2.3 Seeking Support from Each Other

During times of change and transition, it is crucial to lean on each other for support. Be there for your partner emotionally, offering a listening ear and a shoulder to lean on. Validate their feelings and experiences, and remind them that you are in this together. By providing support and understanding, you can strengthen your bond and navigate the challenges of change as a united front.

7.2.4 Maintaining Open Communication

Effective communication is key during times of change and transition. Be proactive in discussing any concerns or fears that arise, and encourage your partner to do the same. By maintaining open lines of communication, you can address any issues that may arise and find solutions together. Remember to listen actively and empathetically, allowing your partner to express their thoughts and feelings without judgment.

7.2.5 Embracing Flexibility and Adaptability

Life changes often require flexibility and adaptability. Be willing to adjust your expectations and plans as needed, understanding that unforeseen circumstances may arise. Embrace the unknown and approach it with a sense of curiosity and adventure. By being flexible and adaptable, you can navigate life changes with resilience and grace.

7.2.6 Taking Care of Yourself and Each Other

During times of change and transition, it is essential to prioritize self-care and care for your partner. Take time to engage in activities that bring you joy and help you recharge. Encourage your partner to do the same. By taking care of yourselves, you can better support each other through the challenges that come with change.

7.2.7 Seeking Professional Help if Needed

Sometimes, life changes and transitions can be particularly challenging, and it may be beneficial to seek professional help. A therapist or counselor can provide guidance and support as you navigate these changes together. They can help you develop coping strategies, improve communication, and strengthen your relationship during times of transition.

7.2.8 Embracing Growth and Learning

Life changes and transitions offer opportunities for personal and relational growth. Embrace the lessons that come with change and view them as opportunities for self-improvement and strengthening your bond. Approach these challenges with a growth mindset, knowing that you and your partner can learn and grow together.

7.2.9 Celebrating Milestones and Achievements

Amidst the challenges of life changes, it is important to celebrate milestones and achievements together. Take time to acknowledge and appreciate the progress you have made as a couple. Celebrate the small victories and remind each other of the strength and resilience you possess.

7.2.10 Embracing the Journey

Remember that life is a journey, and change is a natural part of that journey. Embrace the ups and downs, the twists and turns, and approach them with a sense of adventure and curiosity. By embracing the journey together, you can navigate life changes and transitions with love, compassion, and a deep connection.

Life changes and transitions can be daunting, but with the right skills and mindset, you and your partner can navigate them successfully. By embracing change together, maintaining open communication, and supporting each other, you can strengthen your relationship and emerge stronger on the other side. Remember, change is an opportunity for growth and learning, and by approaching it with love and resilience, you can create a lasting love that withstands the tests of time.

7.3 Supporting Each Other's Personal Growth

In any relationship, personal growth is a vital aspect that contributes to the overall health and longevity of the partnership. When both individuals are committed to their own personal development and support each other in their journey, the relationship becomes a fertile ground for growth and transformation. In this section, we will explore the importance of supporting each other's personal growth and provide practical strategies for fostering growth within the relationship.

7.3.1 Embracing Individuality

One of the fundamental principles of supporting each other's personal growth is embracing and celebrating each other's individuality. Each person in a relationship has their own unique set of dreams, goals, and passions. It is crucial to recognize and honor these individual aspirations, allowing each partner the space and freedom to pursue their personal growth.

Encouraging individuality within the relationship not only fosters personal fulfillment but also enhances the overall connection between partners. When both individuals feel supported and encouraged to explore their own interests and passions, they bring a sense of vitality and excitement into the relationship. This mutual support creates an environment where personal growth can thrive.

7.3.2 Active Listening and Empathy

Supporting each other's personal growth requires active listening and empathy. It is essential to create a safe and non-judgmental space where both partners can openly express their thoughts, feelings, and desires. By actively listening to each other's experiences and perspectives, partners can gain a deeper understanding of each other's personal growth journeys.

Empathy plays a crucial role in supporting personal growth within a relationship. When one partner is going through a period of growth or facing challenges, the other partner can offer empathy and understanding. This support helps create a sense of emotional safety and validation, allowing the individual to explore their personal growth with confidence and resilience.

7.3.3 Setting Goals Together

Setting goals together is a powerful way to support each other's personal growth. By collaboratively identifying shared goals and aspirations, partners can create a roadmap for their individual and collective growth. This process involves open and honest communication, where both partners express their desires and aspirations for personal development.

When setting goals together, it is important to ensure that they align with each partner's values and aspirations. By supporting each other in achieving these goals, partners can provide the necessary motivation, accountability, and encouragement. This shared commitment to personal growth strengthens the bond between partners and creates a sense of unity and purpose within the relationship.

7.3.4 Providing Emotional Support

Emotional support is a cornerstone of supporting each other's personal growth. During times of personal transformation or facing challenges, partners can offer a listening ear, a shoulder to lean on, and words of encouragement. By providing emotional support, partners create a nurturing and safe environment where personal growth can flourish.

It is important to remember that personal growth journeys can be accompanied by moments of vulnerability and self-doubt. As a supportive partner, it is crucial to validate and acknowledge these emotions, offering reassurance and understanding. By being present and empathetic, partners can help each other navigate the ups and downs of personal growth, fostering resilience and strength within the relationship.

7.3.5 Encouraging Self-Care and Self-Reflection

Supporting each other's personal growth involves encouraging self-care and self-reflection. Taking care of one's physical, emotional, and mental well-being is essential for personal growth. Partners can support each other by promoting healthy habits, such as regular exercise, adequate rest, and engaging in activities that bring joy and fulfillment.

Self-reflection is another vital aspect of personal growth. Partners can encourage each other to engage in introspection, self-exploration, and self-awareness. By fostering a culture of self-reflection, partners can gain a deeper understanding of themselves and their personal growth journeys. This self-awareness enhances the quality of the relationship and allows for more meaningful connections.

7.3.6 Celebrating Milestones and Achievements

Celebrating milestones and achievements is an important way to support each other's personal growth. Whether it's completing a challenging project, reaching a personal goal, or overcoming a significant obstacle, partners can celebrate these accomplishments together. By acknowledging and celebrating each other's milestones, partners reinforce the importance of personal growth within the relationship.

Celebrations can take various forms, such as planning a special date night, writing heartfelt letters of appreciation, or organizing a small gathering with loved ones. These gestures of celebration not only show support and pride but also strengthen the bond between partners. By celebrating each other's personal growth, partners create a positive and uplifting environment that encourages continued growth and development.

In conclusion, supporting each other's personal growth is a vital component of a healthy and fulfilling relationship. By embracing individuality, practicing active listening and empathy, setting goals together, providing emotional support, encouraging self-care and self-reflection, and celebrating milestones, partners can create an environment that nurtures personal growth. When both individuals are committed to their own growth and support each other's journeys, the relationship becomes a catalyst for transformation and lasting love.

7.4 Overcoming Relationship Ruts and Plateaus

Relationships are not always smooth sailing. Even the most loving and committed couples can find themselves in ruts or plateaus at times. These periods can be frustrating and disheartening, but they are a normal part of any long-term relationship. The good news is that with the right approach and mindset, you can overcome these challenges and reignite the spark in your relationship.

7.4.1 Recognizing Relationship Ruts and Plateaus

Before we delve into strategies for overcoming relationship ruts and plateaus, it is important to understand what they are and how they can manifest in a relationship. A relationship rut is a period of stagnation or monotony where the excitement and passion seem to have faded away. It may feel like you and your partner are going through the motions without any real connection or growth.

On the other hand, a relationship plateau is a phase where the relationship feels stable and comfortable, but it lacks the excitement and novelty that was present in the earlier stages. While a plateau may not be as distressing as a rut, it can still lead to feelings of complacency and a lack of fulfillment.

Both ruts and plateaus can occur for various reasons, such as a lack of communication, unresolved conflicts, or a loss of shared goals and interests. It is crucial to recognize when your relationship is in a rut or on a plateau so that you can take proactive steps to address the issue.

7.4.2 Open and Honest Communication

One of the most effective ways to overcome relationship ruts and plateaus is through open and honest communication. It is essential to create a safe and non-judgmental space where both partners can express their feelings, concerns, and desires. By openly discussing your emotions and needs, you can gain a deeper understanding of each other and work together to find solutions.

During these conversations, it is important to actively listen to your partner without interrupting or becoming defensive. Validate their feelings and experiences, even if you may not fully understand or agree with them. By showing empathy and understanding, you can foster a sense of emotional connection and create a solid foundation for growth.

7.4.3 Rekindling the Flame

To overcome relationship ruts and plateaus, it is crucial to rekindle the flame of passion and excitement. This can be achieved by introducing novelty and spontaneity into your relationship. Try new activities together, explore new hobbies, or plan surprise date nights. By injecting fresh experiences into your routine, you can reignite the spark and create new memories together.

It is also important to prioritize intimacy and physical affection. Physical touch, such as holding hands, hugging, or cuddling, can help foster a sense of closeness and connection. Additionally, exploring each other's desires and fantasies can add excitement and novelty to your sexual relationship.

7.4.4 Rediscovering Shared Goals and Interests

Another effective strategy for overcoming relationship ruts and plateaus is to rediscover shared goals and interests. As time goes on, it is common for couples to drift apart and lose sight of the things that initially brought them together. Take the time to reflect on your shared values and aspirations, and find ways to align your individual goals with the vision you have for your relationship.

Engaging in activities that you both enjoy and are passionate about can help reignite the sense of camaraderie and shared purpose. Whether it's traveling, volunteering, or pursuing a common hobby, finding ways to connect on a deeper level can help break free from the monotony of a relationship rut or plateau.

7.4.5 Seeking Professional Help

If you find that despite your best efforts, you are still struggling to overcome a relationship rut or plateau, seeking professional help can be beneficial. Relationship therapists or counselors can provide guidance and support in navigating these challenges. They can help you identify underlying issues, improve communication skills, and develop strategies for reconnecting with your partner.

Remember, seeking professional help is not a sign of weakness but rather a proactive step towards strengthening your relationship. A trained therapist can offer valuable insights and tools to help you overcome obstacles and create a more fulfilling and lasting love.

7.4.6 Embracing Growth and Change

Lastly, it is important to embrace growth and change both individually and as a couple. Relationships are dynamic and evolve over time. Embracing personal growth and encouraging your partner to do the same can lead to a deeper connection and a more fulfilling relationship.

Be open to trying new things, learning from past mistakes, and adapting to the changes that life brings. By continuously investing in your personal growth and the growth of your relationship, you can overcome relationship ruts and plateaus and create a love that stands the test of time.

Remember, every relationship goes through ups and downs. It is how you navigate these challenges that determine the strength and longevity of your love. By implementing the strategies discussed in this section and maintaining a commitment to growth and communication, you can overcome relationship ruts and plateaus and create a lasting and fulfilling partnership.

8

Chapter 8

8.1 Building Trust in Relationships

Trust is the foundation upon which strong and lasting relationships are built. It is the glue that holds two people together, allowing them to feel safe, secure, and supported in each other's presence. Without trust, a relationship is like a house built on shaky ground, vulnerable to collapse at any moment. In this section, we will explore the importance of building trust in relationships and provide practical strategies to cultivate trust and security.

The Importance of Trust

Trust is the cornerstone of any successful relationship. It is the belief that you can rely on your partner to be honest, loyal, and supportive. Trust creates a sense of emotional safety and security, allowing both partners to be vulnerable and authentic with each other. When trust is present, it fosters open communication, deepens emotional connection, and strengthens the bond between two individuals.

Building Trust

Building trust in a relationship takes time, effort, and consistent actions. It requires both partners to be committed to nurturing trust and creating a safe space for vulnerability. Here are some strategies to help you build trust in your relationship:

1. Open and Honest Communication

Effective communication is essential for building trust. Be open and honest with your partner about your thoughts, feelings, and concerns. Practice active listening, empathy, and validation to create a safe environment for open dialogue. Avoid withholding information or hiding your true emotions, as this can erode trust over time.

2. Consistency and Reliability

Consistency and reliability are key components of trust. Be consistent in your words and actions, following through on your commitments and promises. Show up for your partner consistently, both in good times and challenging moments. This demonstrates your reliability and builds trust in your relationship.

3. Transparency and Accountability

Transparency and accountability are crucial for building trust. Be open about your intentions, desires, and boundaries. Take responsibility for your actions and apologize when you make mistakes. By being transparent and accountable, you show your partner that you can be trusted and that you value their trust in return.

4. Respect for Boundaries

Respecting each other's boundaries is essential for building trust. Honor your partner's need for personal space, privacy, and autonomy. Avoid crossing boundaries without consent and communicate openly about your own boundaries. Respecting boundaries fosters a sense of safety and trust within the relationship.

5. Building Emotional Connection

Emotional connection is a powerful tool for building trust. Invest time and effort into understanding your partner's emotions, needs, and desires.

Show empathy, compassion, and support during challenging times. By building emotional connection, you create a strong foundation of trust and understanding.

Rebuilding Trust After Betrayal

Betrayal can shatter trust in a relationship, leaving both partners feeling hurt, betrayed, and uncertain about the future. Rebuilding trust after betrayal requires patience, honesty and a commitment to healing. Here are some steps to help you rebuild trust after betrayal:

1. Acknowledge and Validate Feelings

Both partners need to acknowledge and validate their feelings about the betrayal. Allow space for open and honest communication, expressing your emotions without judgment. Validate each other's pain and work towards understanding the underlying causes of the betrayal.

2. Take Responsibility and Apologize

The person who betrayed their partner needs to take responsibility for their actions and offer a sincere apology. This includes acknowledging the hurt caused, expressing remorse, and committing to change. The betrayed partner should also express their feelings and needs, allowing for a dialogue that promotes healing and understanding.

3. Rebuilding Transparency and Accountability

Rebuilding trust requires a commitment to transparency and accountability. The person who betrayed their partner should be willing to be transparent about their actions, whereabouts, and intentions. They should also be accountable for their behavior, taking steps to rebuild trust through consistent actions and open communication.

4. Seek Professional Help if Needed

Rebuilding trust after betrayal can be a challenging process that may require professional guidance. Consider seeking the help of a therapist or counselor who specializes in relationship issues. They can provide valuable insights, tools, and support to navigate the healing process and rebuild trust.

Creating a Secure Attachment

A secure attachment is a vital component of trust and security in a relationship. It is the emotional bond that allows both partners to feel safe, supported, and connected. Here are some ways to cultivate a secure attachment:

1. Emotional Availability

Be emotionally available to your partner by actively listening, empathizing, and validating their emotions. Show genuine interest in their thoughts, feelings, and experiences. By being emotionally available, you create a safe space for vulnerability and deepen the emotional connection.

2. Consistent Support

Offer consistent support to your partner, both in times of joy and hardship. Provide comfort, encouragement, and understanding. Consistent support builds trust and strengthens the bond between partners.

3. Nurture Intimacy

Intimacy is a key aspect of a secure attachment. Nurture emotional and physical intimacy by engaging in activities that foster connection and closeness. This can include sharing quality time, engaging in deep conversations, and expressing affection and love.

4. Practice Empathic Understanding

Empathic understanding is essential for creating a secure attachment. Understanding why someone made a mistake and helps let go of past hurts. Holding onto grudges and resentment hinders the development of trust and security in the relationship. But this must not be forced. It can take a longtime for this process and simply wanting someone to get over a past mistake will entrench feelings of hurt and mistrust. It also sends a signal to the partner you hurt, that your irritated by their feelings, and that this is creating a barrier to you enjoying the relationship. This might take professional help to process everyone's feelings.

Building trust in a relationship is a continuous process that requires effort, commitment, and open communication. By implementing these strategies and fostering a secure attachment, you can create a strong foundation of trust and security that will support your relationship's growth and longevity.

Remember, trust is the bedrock of lasting love, and with dedication and practice, you can cultivate a relationship built on trust and mutual respect.

8.2 Rebuilding Trust After Betrayal

Trust is the foundation of any healthy and lasting relationship. It is the glue that holds two people together, allowing them to feel safe, secure, and connected. However, trust can be easily shattered, especially when betrayal occurs. Whether it's infidelity, lies, or broken promises, rebuilding trust after betrayal is a challenging and delicate process. It requires both partners to be committed, patient, and willing to do the necessary work to heal and restore the trust that has been lost.

Understanding the Impact of Betrayal

Betrayal can have a profound impact on both the individual who has been betrayed and the relationship as a whole. It can lead to feelings of anger, hurt, resentment, and a loss of faith in the other person. The betrayed partner may struggle with trust issues, constantly questioning the sincerity and honesty of their partner. Rebuilding trust requires acknowledging and understanding the depth of the pain caused by the betrayal.

Taking Responsibility and Accountability

The first step in rebuilding trust after betrayal is for the person who has betrayed their partner to take full responsibility for their actions. This means acknowledging the hurt they have caused, expressing genuine remorse, and being accountable for their behavior. It is essential for the betrayer to demonstrate a willingness to change and make amends.

Open and Honest Communication

Rebuilding trust requires open and honest communication between both partners. The betrayed partner needs to express their feelings, concerns, and fears, while the betrayer needs to listen with empathy and understanding. It is crucial for both individuals to be transparent and forthcoming about their thoughts, emotions, and intentions. This level of vulnerability and honesty can help rebuild the foundation of trust.

Patience and Time

Rebuilding trust takes time and patience. It cannot be rushed or forced. Both partners need to be willing to invest the necessary time and effort into the healing process. It is essential to understand that trust is not rebuilt overnight but is a gradual process that requires consistent actions and behaviors over time. Patience is key, as it allows for the rebuilding of trust to occur naturally and organically.

Consistency and Reliability

Consistency and reliability are vital in rebuilding trust. The betrayer needs to demonstrate through their actions that they are trustworthy and reliable. This means following through on commitments, being transparent, and consistently showing up for their partner. Consistency builds a sense of security and reliability, which is crucial for rebuilding trust.

Seeking Professional Help

Rebuilding trust after betrayal can be a complex and challenging journey. In some cases, seeking the guidance of a professional therapist or counselor can be beneficial. A trained professional can provide a safe and neutral space for both partners to explore their feelings, address underlying issues, and learn effective strategies for rebuilding trust. Therapy can offer valuable insights, tools, and support throughout the healing process.

Letting Go

Empathic understanding is a crucial aspect of rebuilding trust. It is important for the betrayed partner to understand the feelings, and emotions of the betrayer. This does not mean forgetting or condoning the betrayal but rather releasing the anger and resentment that can hinder the healing process. It allows both partners to move forward and create a new foundation based on trust and understanding.

Rebuilding Intimacy and Connection

Rebuilding trust also involves rebuilding intimacy and connection within the relationship. This can be achieved through open and honest communication, spending quality time together, and engaging in activities that foster emotional and physical closeness. It is important for both partners to prioritize the relationship and invest in nurturing the bond between them.

Moving Forward with Caution

While rebuilding trust is possible, it is important to approach the process with caution. Both partners need to be aware of their own boundaries and limitations. It is essential to establish clear expectations and boundaries moving forward to prevent future betrayals. Rebuilding trust requires ongoing effort, commitment, and a shared understanding of the importance of trust in the relationship.

Rebuilding trust after betrayal is a challenging journey that requires patience, understanding, and a genuine commitment to change. It is possible to heal and restore trust, but it takes time, effort, and a willingness to confront and address the underlying issues that led to the betrayal. With dedication and a shared commitment to growth, couples can rebuild trust and create a stronger, more resilient relationship.

8.3 Creating a Secure Attachment

Creating a secure attachment is a fundamental aspect of building a strong and lasting relationship. When both partners feel safe, supported, and connected, they can navigate challenges together with confidence and trust. In this section, we will explore the importance of creating a secure attachment and provide practical strategies to cultivate this essential foundation in your relationship.

Understanding Attachment Styles

Attachment styles are deeply ingrained patterns of relating to others that develop early in life. These styles influence how we perceive and respond to our partners' needs, emotions, and behaviors. Understanding your attachment style and your partner's can help you identify potential challenges and develop strategies to create a secure attachment.

There are four main attachment styles:

1. **Secure Attachment**: Individuals with a secure attachment style feel comfortable with intimacy and are able to trust and rely on their partners. They have a positive view of themselves and their relationships, and they effectively communicate their needs and emotions.

2. **Anxious Attachment**: People with an anxious attachment style often worry about their partner's availability and fear rejection or abandonment. They may seek constant reassurance and validation, and their emotions can fluctuate rapidly.

3. **Avoidant Attachment**: Individuals with an avoidant attachment style tend to avoid emotional closeness and may feel uncomfortable with intimacy. They value independence and self-reliance, often suppressing their emotions and distancing themselves from their partners.

4. **Fearful-Avoidant Attachment**: This attachment style combines elements of both anxious and avoidant attachment. People with a fearful-avoidant attachment style desire closeness but also fear rejection and

may struggle with trust and vulnerability.

Cultivating a Secure Attachment

Creating a secure attachment requires intentional effort and a willingness to explore and address any underlying attachment wounds or insecurities. Here are some strategies to help you cultivate a secure attachment in your relationship:

8.3.1 Developing Emotional Availability

Emotional availability is the ability to be present and attuned to your partner's emotions and needs. It involves active listening, empathy, and validation. By practicing emotional availability, you create a safe space for your partner to express themselves and feel understood.

- **Practice active listening**: Give your partner your full attention, maintain eye contact, and show genuine interest in what they are saying. Reflect back their feelings and thoughts to ensure you understand them correctly.
- **Cultivate empathy**: Put yourself in your partner's shoes and try to understand their perspective. Validate their emotions and let them know that you are there to support them.
- **Express appreciation and validation**: Regularly express gratitude for your partner and acknowledge their efforts. Validate their feelings and experiences, even if you may not fully understand or agree with them.

8.3.2 Building Trust and Security

Trust is the foundation of a secure attachment. It involves being reliable, consistent, and transparent in your actions and words. Building trust requires open communication, honesty, and a commitment to follow through on your promises.

- **Communicate openly**: Share your thoughts, feelings, and concerns with your partner. Be honest and transparent about your needs, boundaries, and expectations.

- **Be reliable and consistent**: Follow through on your commitments and be dependable. Show up for your partner consistently and be someone they can rely on.
- **Address past wounds and insecurities**: If you or your partner have experienced past traumas or attachment wounds, seek professional support to heal and work through these issues together. This can help create a stronger foundation of trust and security.

8.3.3 Nurturing Intimacy and Connection

Intimacy and connection are vital components of a secure attachment. They involve creating shared experiences, fostering emotional and physical closeness, and prioritizing quality time together.

- **Prioritize quality time**: Set aside dedicated time to connect with your partner. Engage in activities that you both enjoy and create opportunities for meaningful conversations and shared experiences.
- **Express love and affection**: Show your partner love and affection through physical touch, verbal affirmations, and acts of kindness. Small gestures can go a long way in nurturing intimacy and connection.
- **Explore emotional and physical intimacy**: Continuously explore and deepen your emotional and physical connection. Be open to trying new things, expressing your desires, and understanding your partner's needs.

Conclusion

Creating a secure attachment is essential for building a strong and lasting relationship. By understanding your attachment style and implementing strategies to cultivate a secure attachment, you and your partner can create a foundation of trust, safety, and emotional connection. Remember, building a secure attachment takes time and effort, but the rewards of a healthy and fulfilling relationship are well worth it.

8.4 Fostering Emotional Safety

Emotional safety is a crucial aspect of any healthy and lasting relationship. It creates an environment where both partners feel secure, supported, and free to express themselves authentically. When emotional safety is present, individuals can open up, be vulnerable, and trust that their partner will respond with empathy and understanding. In this section, we will explore the importance of fostering emotional safety in your relationship and provide practical strategies to cultivate it.

8.4.1 Understanding Emotional Safety

Emotional safety refers to the sense of security and comfort that individuals experience within their relationship. It involves creating an atmosphere where both partners feel accepted, respected, and valued for who they are. When emotional safety is present, individuals can freely express their thoughts, feelings, and needs without fear of judgment, rejection, or criticism.

In contrast, a lack of emotional safety can lead to feelings of insecurity, anxiety, and defensiveness. It can hinder effective communication, intimacy, and trust within the relationship. Without emotional safety, individuals may hesitate to share their true selves, leading to a lack of authenticity and emotional connection.

8.4.2 Building Emotional Safety

Building emotional safety requires intentional effort and a commitment to creating a nurturing and supportive environment for both partners. Here are some strategies to foster emotional safety in your relationship:

8.4.2.1 Cultivate Open and Honest Communication

Effective communication is the foundation of emotional safety. Encourage open and honest dialogue by creating a safe space for both partners to express their thoughts and feelings without fear of judgment or criticism. Practice active listening, empathy, and validation to ensure that your partner feels heard and understood. Avoid interrupting or dismissing their concerns, and instead, strive to validate their experiences and emotions.

8.4.2.2 Practice Non-Defensive Responding

When conflicts or disagreements arise, it is essential to respond in a non-defensive manner. Avoid becoming defensive or reactive when your partner expresses their concerns or frustrations. Instead, strive to understand their perspective and validate their feelings. Responding with empathy and compassion can help diffuse tension and create an atmosphere of emotional safety.

8.4.2.3 Respect Boundaries and Autonomy

Respecting each other's boundaries and autonomy is crucial for fostering emotional safety. Recognize and honor your partner's need for personal space, privacy, and independence. Avoid controlling or manipulating behaviors and allow each other the freedom to make individual choices. By respecting boundaries, you demonstrate trust and create an environment where both partners feel safe to be themselves.

8.4.2.4 Build Trust and Reliability

Trust is a fundamental component of emotional safety. Foster trust within your relationship by being reliable and consistent in your words and actions. Follow through on your commitments and promises, and be transparent and honest with your partner. Trust is built over time through consistent behaviors that demonstrate reliability and integrity.

8.4.2.5 Validate and Empathize

Validation and empathy are powerful tools for creating emotional safety. Validate your partner's emotions and experiences by acknowledging their feelings and expressing understanding. Avoid dismissing or minimizing their concerns, as this can erode emotional safety. Practice empathy by putting yourself in their shoes and seeking to understand their perspective. By validating and empathizing, you create an environment where both partners feel valued and supported.

8.4.2.6 Foster Emotional Intimacy

Emotional intimacy is closely linked to emotional safety. Cultivate emotional intimacy by sharing your thoughts, feelings, and vulnerabilities with your partner. Create opportunities for deep conversations and meaningful connections. By fostering emotional intimacy, you strengthen the bond between you and your partner, creating a sense of safety and security.

8.4.2.7 Prioritize Self-Care and Self-Reflection

Taking care of your own emotional well-being is essential for fostering emotional safety in your relationship. Engage in self-care activities that promote your mental, emotional, and physical health. Practice self-reflection to gain insight into your own triggers, patterns, and behaviors that may impact the emotional safety of the relationship. By prioritizing self-care and self-reflection, you can show up as a more emotionally available and secure partner.

8.4.3 Overcoming Emotional Safety Challenges

Fostering emotional safety is an ongoing process that requires effort and commitment from both partners. However, challenges may arise along the way. Here are some common challenges and strategies to overcome them:

8.4.3.1 Addressing Past Trauma

Past trauma can significantly impact emotional safety within a relationship. If you or your partner have experienced trauma, it is crucial to seek professional support and therapy to address and heal from these wounds. Trauma-informed therapy can provide tools and strategies to navigate the impact of past trauma on emotional safety.

8.4.3.2 Managing Insecurities and Jealousy

Insecurities and jealousy can undermine emotional safety. It is important to address these emotions openly and honestly with your partner. Practice self-reflection to understand the root causes of these feelings and communicate your needs and concerns to your partner. Together, you can work on building trust, reassurance, and understanding to overcome insecurities and jealousy.

8.4.3.3 Seeking Couples Therapy

If you find it challenging to foster emotional safety in your relationship, couples therapy can be a valuable resource. A trained therapist can provide guidance, support, and tools to help you and your partner navigate emotional safety challenges. Couples therapy can offer a safe and neutral space to address underlying issues and work towards building a more emotionally secure relationship.

Conclusion

Fostering emotional safety is essential for creating a healthy and lasting relationship. By cultivating open communication, respect, trust, validation, and empathy, you can create an environment where both partners feel secure, supported, and free to be their authentic selves. Remember that building emotional safety is an ongoing process that requires effort, commitment, and a willingness to grow together as a couple. With the right skills and dedication, you can create a relationship that is emotionally safe, fulfilling, and resilient.

9

Chapter 9

9.Balancing Independence and Togetherness

9.1 Maintaining Individual Identities

Maintaining individual identities is a crucial aspect of any healthy and lasting relationship. While it is natural for two people in a relationship to become intertwined and share many aspects of their lives, it is equally important for each individual to maintain their own sense of self and personal identity. This section will explore the significance of maintaining individual identities in a relationship and provide practical strategies for achieving this balance.

The Importance of Individual Identities

In the journey of love and partnership, it can be easy to lose sight of our own individuality. We may become so consumed by the relationship that we neglect our own needs, interests, and passions. However, maintaining a strong sense of self is vital for personal growth, fulfillment, and overall relationship satisfaction.

1. **Self-Discovery and Personal Growth:** By maintaining our individual identities, we create space for self-discovery and personal growth. It allows us to explore our own interests, pursue our passions, and develop a deeper understanding of ourselves. This self-awareness not only enriches our own lives but also enhances the quality of our relationship.

2. **Autonomy and Independence:** Maintaining individual identities fosters a sense of autonomy and independence within the relationship. It allows each partner to have their own space, make independent decisions, and have a sense of control over their own lives. This autonomy not only promotes personal well-being but also contributes to a healthier dynamic within the relationship.

3. **Enhanced Attraction and Desire:** When both partners maintain their individual identities, it can actually enhance attraction and desire within the relationship. The unique qualities, interests, and experiences that each individual brings to the table create a sense of intrigue and excitement. This continuous growth and self-improvement can reignite the spark and keep the relationship dynamic and vibrant.

Strategies for Maintaining Individual Identities

While it is essential to prioritize the relationship, it is equally important to nurture and maintain our own individual identities. Here are some practical strategies to help achieve this balance:

1. **Open Communication:** Establish open and honest communication with your partner about the importance of maintaining individual identities. Discuss your personal goals, interests, and the need for personal space. By having these conversations, you can ensure that both partners are on the same page and understand the significance of this aspect of the relationship.

2. **Set Boundaries:** Establish clear boundaries that respect each other's autonomy and personal space. This may include having designated alone time, pursuing individual hobbies or interests, and respecting

each other's need for independence. By setting boundaries, you create a healthy framework that allows both partners to maintain their individual identities while still being committed to the relationship.

3. **Support Each Other's Passions:** Encourage and support each other's passions and interests. Take an active interest in your partner's hobbies and endeavors, and be their biggest cheerleader. By showing genuine support and enthusiasm, you not only strengthen the bond between you but also create an environment that nurtures individual growth and fulfillment.

4. **Maintain a Supportive Network:** Cultivate a supportive network of friends, family, and mentors outside of the relationship. Having a strong support system provides additional sources of emotional support, guidance, and inspiration. It also allows you to engage in activities and conversations that are separate from the relationship, further nurturing your individual identity.

5. **Practice Self-Care:** Prioritize self-care and self-reflection as part of your routine. Engage in activities that bring you joy, practice mindfulness or meditation, and take time for self-reflection. By investing in your own well-being, you are better equipped to bring your best self to the relationship.

Embracing Togetherness and Individuality

Maintaining individual identities does not mean neglecting the relationship or distancing oneself from the partner. It is about finding a healthy balance between togetherness and individuality. When both partners prioritize their personal growth and fulfillment, it creates a strong foundation for a thriving and lasting relationship.

Remember, a healthy relationship is not about losing oneself in the process but rather about growing together while honoring each other's individuality. By maintaining your own identity, you bring a unique and valuable contribution to the relationship, fostering a deep sense of connection and mutual respect.

In the next section, we will explore the importance of creating shared goals and dreams in a relationship, further enhancing the bond between partners while maintaining individual identities.

Please note that the content provided here is a sample and should be used as a reference. The actual content may vary based on the specific needs and requirements of the book.

9.2 Creating Shared Goals and Dreams

Creating shared goals and dreams is an essential aspect of building a strong and lasting relationship. When two individuals come together, they bring their unique aspirations, desires, and ambitions. By aligning these individual goals and dreams, couples can create a shared vision for their future, fostering a sense of unity and purpose.

9.2.1 The Power of Shared Goals and Dreams

Shared goals and dreams serve as a guiding force in a relationship, providing a sense of direction and purpose. When couples have a common vision for their future, it strengthens their bond and creates a strong foundation for their relationship. It allows them to work together towards a common objective, fostering a sense of teamwork and collaboration.

Having shared goals and dreams also helps couples to stay focused and motivated during challenging times. When faced with obstacles or setbacks, having a clear vision of what they want to achieve together can provide the necessary motivation to overcome difficulties and persevere.

9.2.2 Identifying and Aligning Goals and Dreams

To create shared goals and dreams, it is important for each individual to first identify their own personal goals and dreams. This self-reflection allows individuals to gain clarity about what they truly want in life and what brings them fulfillment. It is essential for both partners to have a deep understanding of their own aspirations before they can align them with their partner's.

Once individual goals and dreams are identified, couples can then come together to discuss and align their visions for the future. This process involves open and honest communication, where both partners share their desires and aspirations. It is important to listen actively and validate each other's dreams, creating a safe and supportive environment for open dialogue.

During this process, it is crucial to find common ground and areas of overlap between individual goals and dreams. Identifying shared values, interests, and passions can help couples find common goals that they can work towards together. It is also important to recognize and respect each other's individual goals and dreams that may not align completely, finding a balance between shared aspirations and personal growth.

9.2.3 Setting SMART Goals

Once shared goals and dreams are identified, it is important to set specific, measurable, achievable, relevant, and time-bound (SMART) goals. SMART goals provide a clear roadmap for couples to follow, ensuring that their efforts are focused and purposeful.

Specific goals outline exactly what needs to be achieved, leaving no room for ambiguity. Measurable goals allow couples to track their progress and celebrate milestones along the way. Achievable goals are realistic and within reach, considering the resources and capabilities of both partners. Relevant goals are aligned with the shared vision and values of the relationship. Time-bound goals have a specific deadline or timeframe, providing a sense of urgency and accountability.

By setting SMART goals, couples can break down their shared vision into actionable steps, making it easier to navigate the path towards their dreams. Regularly reviewing and reassessing these goals allows couples to stay on track and make necessary adjustments as they grow and evolve together.

9.2.4 Supporting Each Other's Goals and Dreams

Creating shared goals and dreams does not mean sacrificing individual aspirations. It is important for couples to support and encourage each other's personal goals and dreams alongside their shared vision. By nurturing individual growth and development, couples can create a harmonious balance between independence and togetherness.

Supporting each other's goals and dreams involves actively listening, offering encouragement, and providing practical assistance when needed. It requires a genuine interest in each other's passions and a willingness to celebrate each other's achievements. By being each other's biggest cheerleaders, couples can create a nurturing and empowering environment that fosters personal and shared growth.

9.2.5 Revisiting and Evolving Shared Goals and Dreams

As individuals and relationships evolve over time, it is important to revisit and reassess shared goals and dreams. Life circumstances, personal growth, and external factors may influence the direction of a relationship. Regularly checking in with each other and evaluating the relevance and alignment of shared goals ensures that the relationship remains dynamic and adaptable.

Revisiting shared goals and dreams also provides an opportunity for couples to celebrate their achievements and milestones. It allows them to reflect on their journey together and appreciate the progress they have made. By acknowledging and celebrating their shared accomplishments, couples can strengthen their bond and reinforce their commitment to each other.

In conclusion, creating shared goals and dreams is a vital component of building a strong and lasting relationship. It provides couples with a sense of purpose, unity, and direction. By identifying and aligning individual aspirations, setting SMART goals, supporting each other's dreams, and regularly revisiting and evolving shared goals, couples can cultivate a relationship that thrives on shared vision and mutual growth.

9.3 Supporting Each Other's Passions and Hobbies

In a healthy and thriving relationship, it is essential to support and encourage each other's passions and hobbies. When you and your partner are able to pursue your individual interests and find fulfillment outside of the relationship, it can enhance your overall happiness and strengthen the bond you share. Supporting each other's passions and hobbies not only allows for personal growth and self-expression but also fosters a sense of independence and autonomy within the relationship.

9.3.1 Embracing Individuality

One of the key aspects of supporting each other's passions and hobbies is embracing and celebrating each other's individuality. Recognize that you and your partner are unique individuals with different interests, talents, and aspirations. Encourage each other to explore and pursue these passions, even if they may not align with your own. By doing so, you create a space that allows for personal growth and self-discovery, which can ultimately contribute to a more fulfilling and well-rounded relationship.

9.3.2 Active Interest and Engagement

Supporting each other's passions and hobbies goes beyond simply acknowledging their existence. It involves actively showing interest and engaging in conversations about these pursuits. Take the time to learn about your partner's hobbies, ask questions, and genuinely listen to their experiences and achievements. This not only demonstrates your support but also deepens your connection by fostering a sense of understanding and shared enthusiasm.

9.3.3 Encouragement and Motivation

As partners, it is crucial to be each other's biggest cheerleaders. Encourage and motivate your partner to pursue their passions and hobbies, especially during challenging times. Offer words of encouragement, provide constructive feedback, and celebrate their accomplishments. By being a source of support and inspiration, you create an environment that nurtures personal growth and fosters a sense of confidence and self-belief.

9.3.4 Participating and Collaborating

Supporting each other's passions and hobbies can also involve actively participating and collaborating in these activities. Find opportunities to engage in shared interests or explore new hobbies together. This not only allows you to spend quality time together but also strengthens your bond by creating shared experiences and memories. Collaborating on projects or engaging in joint activities can also foster teamwork, communication, and problem-solving skills within the relationship.

9.3.5 Balancing Time and Priorities

While supporting each other's passions and hobbies is important, it is equally crucial to strike a balance between individual pursuits and shared time as a couple. Open and honest communication about your needs and priorities is essential in finding this balance. Discuss and establish boundaries that allow for both personal growth and quality time together. By respecting each other's needs and finding a healthy equilibrium, you can ensure that both individual and shared interests are nurtured within the relationship.

9.3.6 Overcoming Challenges

Supporting each other's passions and hobbies may come with its own set of challenges. Conflicts may arise when interests clash or when one partner feels neglected due to excessive time spent on individual pursuits. It is important to address these challenges openly and honestly, with empathy and understanding. Seek compromise and find creative solutions that allow both partners to feel supported and fulfilled. Remember that the goal is to create an environment where both individuals can thrive and grow, both individually and as a couple.

9.3.7 Celebrating Achievements

Lastly, celebrating each other's achievements is a vital part of supporting each other's passions and hobbies. Acknowledge and celebrate milestones, big or small, and express genuine pride and joy in your partner's accomplishments. By celebrating each other's successes, you reinforce a positive and supportive dynamic within the relationship, fostering a sense of appreciation and gratitude.

In conclusion, supporting each other's passions and hobbies is an integral aspect of a healthy and fulfilling relationship. Embracing individuality, showing active interest and engagement, providing encouragement and motivation, participating and collaborating, balancing time and priorities, overcoming challenges, and celebrating achievements are all essential components of this support. By nurturing and supporting each other's personal growth and self-expression, you can create a strong foundation for a lasting and loving partnership.

9.4 Finding a Healthy Balance in Time Spent Together

Finding a healthy balance in the time spent together is crucial for maintaining a strong and fulfilling relationship. While spending quality time with your partner is important for building intimacy and connection, it is equally important to maintain a sense of independence and individuality. In this section, we will explore the significance of finding a healthy balance in time spent together and provide practical tips on how to achieve it.

9.4.1 Understanding the Importance of Balance

Finding a healthy balance in the time spent together is essential for the overall well-being of both individuals in a relationship. It allows each partner to maintain their own identity, pursue personal interests, and nurture their own emotional and physical well-being. When individuals have a sense of independence and fulfillment outside of the relationship, they bring more to the partnership and can contribute to its growth and longevity.

On the other hand, spending excessive time together can lead to feelings of suffocation, loss of personal space, and a lack of individual growth. It is important to recognize that both partners need time for self-care, personal reflection, and pursuing their own passions and hobbies. By finding a healthy balance, couples can create a harmonious dynamic that supports both their individual needs and the needs of the relationship.

9.4.2 Communicating and Negotiating Time

Open and honest communication is key when it comes to finding a healthy balance in time spent together. It is important for both partners to express their needs, desires, and boundaries regarding the amount of time they would like to spend together and apart. This communication should be done in a non-confrontational and understanding manner, allowing both partners to feel heard and respected.

Negotiating time can involve creating a schedule or routine that allows for designated alone time and shared activities. It is important to be flexible and adaptable, as individual needs and circumstances may change over time. Regular check-ins and discussions about time spent together can help ensure that both partners feel satisfied and fulfilled in the relationship.

9.4.3 Quality over Quantity

When it comes to spending time together, it is important to prioritize quality over quantity. Instead of focusing solely on the amount of time spent together, focus on the quality of the interactions and the level of connection and intimacy that is fostered. Engaging in meaningful conversations, shared experiences, and activities that bring joy and fulfillment to both partners can create a deeper bond and strengthen the relationship.

It is also important to recognize that quality time can be achieved in various ways. It doesn't always have to involve grand gestures or extravagant outings. Simple acts of kindness, such as cooking a meal together, going for a walk, or engaging in a shared hobby, can create meaningful moments of connection and intimacy.

9.4.4 Nurturing Individual Growth

Finding a healthy balance in time spent together also involves nurturing individual growth and personal development. Encouraging and supporting each other's passions, hobbies, and personal goals can contribute to a sense of fulfillment and happiness outside of the relationship. This not only enhances the individual's well-being but also brings new experiences and perspectives into the partnership.

By fostering a supportive environment that values personal growth, couples can create a strong foundation for their relationship. This includes respecting each other's need for alone time, encouraging self-reflection, and providing emotional support during times of personal growth and exploration.

9.4.5 Reevaluating and Adjusting

Finding a healthy balance in time spent together is an ongoing process that requires regular reevaluation and adjustment. As individuals and circumstances change, it is important to reassess the needs and desires of both partners. This may involve revisiting the agreed-upon schedule, discussing any changes in personal priorities, and ensuring that both partners feel satisfied and fulfilled in the relationship.

Flexibility and open-mindedness are key in maintaining a healthy balance. It is important to be willing to adapt and make compromises when necessary, while also advocating for one's own needs and boundaries. By continuously working together to find a balance that works for both partners, couples can create a relationship that is built on mutual respect, understanding, and support.

Finding a healthy balance in time spent together is essential for creating a strong and fulfilling relationship. By prioritizing open communication, nurturing individual growth, and regularly reevaluating and adjusting, couples can create a harmonious dynamic that allows for both togetherness and independence. Remember, a healthy relationship is one that allows both partners to thrive as individuals while also fostering a deep and meaningful connection.

10

Chapter 10

10.Sustaining Long-Term Love

10.1 Keeping the Spark Alive

In the journey of sustaining a long-term love, one of the most important aspects is keeping the spark alive. It is natural for relationships to go through ups and downs, and it takes effort and intention to maintain the passion and connection that initially brought you together. This section will explore various strategies and practices that can help you nurture the flame of love and keep it burning bright.

10.1.1 Cultivating Emotional Intimacy

Emotional intimacy forms the foundation of a strong and lasting relationship. It is the deep connection that allows you to truly understand and support each other on a profound level. To keep the spark alive, it is crucial to continue cultivating emotional intimacy throughout your journey together.

One way to foster emotional intimacy is through open and honest communication. Take the time to regularly check in with each other, sharing your thoughts, feelings, and desires. Create a safe space where both partners feel comfortable expressing themselves without fear of judgment or criticism. Active listening and validation play a vital role in this process, as they demonstrate your commitment to understanding and empathizing with each other's experiences.

Another powerful tool for cultivating emotional intimacy is practicing gratitude and appreciation. Take the time to acknowledge and express gratitude for the qualities, actions, and efforts that you admire and value in your partner. This practice not only strengthens the bond between you but also helps shift your focus towards the positive aspects of your relationship.

10.1.2 Nurturing Physical Intimacy

Physical intimacy is an essential component of a romantic relationship. It encompasses not only sexual connection but also non-sexual touch, affection, and closeness. To keep the spark alive, it is important to prioritize and nurture physical intimacy in your relationship.

Explore ways to enhance your sexual connection by openly discussing your desires, fantasies, and boundaries. Experiment with new experiences and techniques that can reignite the passion and excitement in the bedroom. Remember that communication and consent are key in maintaining a healthy and fulfilling sexual relationship.

Beyond sexual intimacy, non-sexual touch and affection are equally important in sustaining the spark. Engage in small gestures of physical affection, such as holding hands, hugging, or cuddling. These acts of intimacy can help reinforce the emotional bond between you and create a sense of security and closeness.

10.1.3 Continuing Personal Growth

As individuals, we are constantly evolving and growing. To keep the spark alive in your relationship, it is essential to continue your personal growth journey together. Encourage each other to pursue individual passions, interests, and goals. Support each other's personal development and celebrate the achievements and milestones along the way.

Additionally, fostering a growth mindset within your relationship can contribute to its longevity. Embrace challenges and setbacks as opportunities for learning and growth. Approach conflicts and disagreements with a willingness to understand each other's perspectives and find mutually beneficial solutions. By continuously evolving and adapting together, you can keep the spark alive and create a dynamic and fulfilling partnership.

10.1.4 Creating Meaningful Rituals and Traditions

Rituals and traditions can add depth and meaning to your relationship, creating a sense of shared history and connection. Establishing rituals can be as simple as having a weekly date night or as elaborate as celebrating anniversaries in a special way. These rituals provide opportunities to reconnect, reminisce, and create new memories together.

In addition to established rituals, it is important to create space for spontaneity and adventure. Surprise each other with thoughtful gestures or plan spontaneous outings to keep the excitement alive. By infusing your relationship with a sense of novelty and surprise, you can reignite the spark and prevent complacency from settling in.

10.1.5 Prioritizing Quality Time

In the midst of busy lives and responsibilities, it is crucial to prioritize quality time with your partner. Set aside dedicated time to connect and engage with each other without distractions. This can involve activities such as going for walks, having deep conversations, or engaging in shared hobbies and interests.

During this quality time, make a conscious effort to be fully present and attentive to each other. Put away electronic devices, actively listen, and show genuine interest in your partner's thoughts and experiences. By creating a space for deep connection and meaningful interactions, you can nurture the spark and strengthen your bond.

In conclusion, keeping the spark alive in a long-term relationship requires ongoing effort, intention, and the cultivation of emotional and physical intimacy. By prioritizing emotional connection, nurturing physical intimacy, continuing personal growth, creating meaningful rituals, and prioritizing quality time, you can sustain the passion and love that brought you together. Remember, relationships are a journey, and with the right skills and mindset, you can create a lasting and fulfilling love.

10.2 Continuing to Grow and Evolve Together

In order to sustain a long-term, fulfilling relationship, it is essential for both partners to continue growing and evolving together. Relationships are not static; they require ongoing effort and commitment to adapt to the changes and challenges that life brings. Just as individuals grow and change over time, so do relationships. By actively nurturing personal growth and fostering a shared journey of development, couples can create a strong foundation for lasting love.

10.2.1 Embracing Personal Growth

Personal growth is a lifelong journey that involves self-reflection, self-awareness, and a willingness to learn and evolve. It is important for each partner to prioritize their own growth and development, as this contributes to the overall health and vitality of the relationship. By continuously working on themselves, individuals can bring their best selves to the partnership and create a positive ripple effect.

To embrace personal growth within a relationship, it is crucial to cultivate self-reflection. This involves taking the time to examine one's thoughts, emotions, and behaviors, and to identify areas for improvement. By being open to feedback and self-evaluation, individuals can gain valuable insights into their strengths and weaknesses, and actively work towards personal growth.

Furthermore, developing emotional intelligence is key to sustaining long-term love. Emotional intelligence encompasses the ability to understand and manage one's own emotions, as well as to empathize and connect with others on a deeper level. By honing emotional intelligence skills, individuals can enhance their communication, resolve conflicts more effectively, and foster greater intimacy within the relationship.

10.2.2 Cultivating Shared Growth

While personal growth is important, it is equally vital for couples to cultivate shared growth within their relationship. This involves setting goals and aspirations together, and actively working towards them as a team. By aligning their visions for the future, couples can create a sense of purpose and direction, which strengthens their bond and fosters a deeper connection.

One powerful way to cultivate shared growth is by engaging in regular check-ins and conversations about individual and shared goals. This allows partners to support each other's aspirations, provide encouragement, and hold each other accountable. By actively participating in each other's growth journeys, couples can create a sense of unity and shared purpose.

Additionally, supporting each other's passions and hobbies is crucial for sustaining long-term love. Encouraging and celebrating each other's individual interests not only fosters personal growth, but also strengthens the bond between partners. By showing genuine interest and involvement in each other's pursuits, couples can create a sense of mutual support and admiration.

10.2.3 Embracing Change and Adaptation

As individuals and as a couple, it is important to embrace change and adapt to the evolving circumstances of life. Relationships are not immune to challenges and transitions, and it is essential to approach them with a growth mindset. By viewing challenges as opportunities for growth and learning, couples can navigate them together and emerge stronger on the other side.

One key aspect of embracing change is maintaining open and honest communication. By expressing one's needs, concerns, and desires, couples can work together to find solutions and make necessary adjustments. It is important to approach these conversations with empathy, understanding, and a willingness to compromise.

Furthermore, celebrating milestones and anniversaries is a powerful way to acknowledge and appreciate the growth and progress within the relationship. By commemorating important moments, couples can reflect on their journey together and express gratitude for the love and connection they have built. These celebrations serve as reminders of the commitment and dedication invested in the relationship, and provide motivation to continue growing and evolving together.

10.2.4 Navigating the Challenges of Long-Term Commitment

Long-term commitment requires resilience, patience, and a willingness to work through challenges. It is inevitable that couples will face difficulties along the way, but it is how they navigate these challenges that determines the strength and longevity of their love.

One important aspect of navigating challenges is maintaining a strong emotional connection. By prioritizing quality time together, engaging in meaningful conversations, and expressing love and appreciation, couples can strengthen their bond and weather the storms that come their way. It is crucial to create a safe and supportive space where both partners feel heard, understood, and valued.

Additionally, seeking support from trusted friends, family, or professionals can be invaluable during challenging times. Sometimes, an outside perspective or guidance can provide fresh insights and strategies for overcoming obstacles. It is important to remember that seeking help is not a sign of weakness, but rather a proactive step towards nurturing the relationship.

In conclusion, sustaining long-term love requires a commitment to personal growth, shared growth, embracing change, and navigating challenges with resilience and dedication. By continuing to grow and evolve together, couples can create a relationship that not only withstands the test of time but also thrives in the face of adversity. Love is a journey, and by actively investing in the growth and development of the relationship, couples can create a lasting and fulfilling partnership.

10.3 Navigating the Challenges of Long-Term Commitment

Long-term commitment in a relationship can be both rewarding and challenging. It is a journey that requires dedication, effort, and the willingness to navigate through various obstacles that may arise along the way. In this section, we will explore some of the common challenges that couples face in long-term commitment and provide strategies to overcome them.

10.3.1 Maintaining Individuality within the Relationship

One of the challenges in long-term commitment is finding a healthy balance between independence and togetherness. As individuals, we have our own unique identities, passions, and interests. It is important to maintain a sense of self within the relationship while also fostering a strong connection with your partner.

To navigate this challenge, it is crucial to communicate openly and honestly with your partner about your needs for personal space and time. Encourage each other to pursue individual hobbies, interests, and goals. By supporting each other's individual growth and maintaining a sense of independence, you can strengthen the foundation of your relationship.

10.3.2 Managing Routine and Monotony

Over time, relationships can fall into a routine, which may lead to feelings of monotony and boredom. It is important to actively work on keeping the spark alive and injecting excitement into your relationship.

One way to navigate this challenge is by introducing novelty and spontaneity into your daily lives. Plan surprise dates, explore new activities together, or take spontaneous weekend getaways. Additionally, regularly communicate with your partner about your desires and fantasies, and be open to trying new things together. By continuously seeking new experiences and maintaining a sense of adventure, you can prevent the relationship from becoming stagnant.

10.3.3 Dealing with Changing Needs and Priorities

As individuals grow and evolve, their needs and priorities may change. This can create challenges in a long-term commitment, as both partners may need to adapt to these changes.

To navigate this challenge, it is essential to have open and honest communication about your evolving needs and priorities. Regularly check in with each other to ensure that you are both on the same page and willing to support each other's growth. Flexibility, understanding, and compromise are key in navigating the changing dynamics of a long-term commitment.

10.3.4 Overcoming Relationship Ruts and Plateaus

Relationships go through ups and downs, and it is common to experience periods of stagnation or plateau. During these times, it is important to actively work on reigniting the passion and connection in your relationship.

To navigate this challenge, prioritize quality time together and engage in activities that foster emotional and physical intimacy. Plan regular date nights, engage in deep conversations, and express appreciation and gratitude for each other. Additionally, consider seeking professional help, such as couples therapy or relationship coaching, to gain new perspectives and tools for overcoming relationship ruts.

10.3.5 Managing External Influences and Interference

External influences, such as family, friends, and societal expectations, can pose challenges in a long-term commitment. These influences may create conflicts, misunderstandings, or pressure on the relationship.

To navigate this challenge, it is important to establish clear boundaries and communicate openly with your partner about your needs and concerns. Discuss how you can support each other in managing external influences and interference. Remember that your relationship is unique, and it is essential to prioritize your own happiness and well-being above external expectations.

10.3.6 Cultivating Emotional Safety and Trust

Emotional safety and trust are the foundation of a healthy and lasting relationship. However, they can be challenged by past traumas, insecurities, or breaches of trust.

To navigate this challenge, it is crucial to create a safe and supportive environment for open and honest communication. Practice active listening, empathy, and validation to foster emotional safety. Additionally, work on rebuilding trust if it has been damaged, through transparency, consistency, and accountability. Seeking professional help, such as individual or couples therapy, can also be beneficial in healing past wounds and strengthening emotional safety and trust.

10.3.7 Embracing Growth and Evolution

Individual growth and evolution are natural processes that occur throughout life. In a long-term commitment, it is important to embrace these changes and support each other's personal development.

To navigate this challenge, encourage and celebrate each other's growth and achievements. Be open to learning and evolving together as a couple. Regularly communicate about your goals, dreams, and aspirations, and find ways to support each other in pursuing them. By embracing growth and evolution, you can create a relationship that continues to thrive and deepen over time.

Navigating the challenges of long-term commitment requires dedication, effort, and a willingness to adapt and grow. By actively addressing these challenges and implementing strategies to overcome them, you can create a strong and fulfilling relationship that stands the test of time. Remember, relationships are a continuous journey of learning and growth, and with the right skills and mindset, you can sustain lasting love.

11

Chapter 11

11.Overcoming Relationship Obstacles

11.1 Dealing with Jealousy and Insecurity

Jealousy and insecurity can be common challenges in relationships, regardless of sexual orientation. These emotions can arise from a variety of sources, such as past experiences, fear of abandonment, or a lack of self-confidence. In lesbian and queer relationships, these feelings may be compounded by societal pressures and stereotypes, which can further contribute to feelings of inadequacy or fear of losing a partner.

It is important to recognize that jealousy and insecurity are normal human emotions. However, when left unchecked, they can have a detrimental impact on the health and longevity of a relationship. Learning how to effectively deal with these emotions is crucial for creating a strong and lasting bond with your partner.

Understanding the Root Causes

To effectively address jealousy and insecurity, it is important to understand their root causes. These emotions often stem from deep-seated fears and insecurities within ourselves. They can be triggered by a variety of factors, such as past relationship traumas, feelings of inadequacy, or a fear of rejection.

In lesbian and queer relationships, societal pressures and stereotypes can also contribute to feelings of jealousy and insecurity. For example, the fear of being compared to societal beauty standards or the fear of losing a partner to societal expectations can intensify these emotions.

Building Self-Confidence and Self-Worth

One of the most effective ways to combat jealousy and insecurity is by building self-confidence and self-worth. When we have a strong sense of self and believe in our own value, we are less likely to feel threatened by external factors or compare ourselves to others.

To build self-confidence and self-worth, it is important to engage in self-reflection and personal growth. This can involve identifying and challenging negative self-beliefs, practicing self-care, and setting boundaries that prioritize your own well-being. Additionally, surrounding yourself with a supportive community of friends and loved ones can help boost your self-esteem and provide a sense of validation.

Open and Honest Communication

Open and honest communication is essential for addressing jealousy and insecurity within a relationship. It is important to create a safe and non-judgmental space where both partners can express their fears and concerns without fear of retribution.

When discussing feelings of jealousy or insecurity, it is crucial to use "I" statements and focus on expressing your own emotions rather than blaming or accusing your partner. This allows for a more productive and empathetic conversation, where both partners can work together to find solutions and provide reassurance.

Trust and Transparency

Building trust and transparency within a relationship is vital for overcoming jealousy and insecurity. Trust is the foundation upon which a healthy relationship is built, and it requires both partners to be open, honest, and reliable.

To foster trust, it is important to be consistent in your words and actions. Follow through on your commitments, be reliable, and communicate openly about your feelings and intentions. Additionally, it is important to establish clear boundaries and expectations within the relationship, ensuring that both partners feel secure and respected.

Seeking Professional Help

In some cases, addressing jealousy and insecurity may require the assistance of a professional therapist or counselor. A trained professional can provide guidance and support in navigating these complex emotions and help both partners develop effective coping strategies.

Therapy can also provide a safe space for exploring the underlying causes of jealousy and insecurity, allowing for deeper self-reflection and personal growth. Through therapy, individuals can gain a better understanding of their emotions and develop healthier ways of managing and expressing them within their relationship.

Cultivating Self-Compassion

Lastly, it is important to cultivate self-compassion when dealing with jealousy and insecurity. Remember that these emotions are normal and do not define your worth or the success of your relationship. Be kind to yourself and practice self-care during times of heightened emotions.

By practicing self-compassion, you can learn to acknowledge and validate your feelings without allowing them to consume you. This allows for a healthier and more balanced approach to addressing jealousy and insecurity within your relationship.

Remember, overcoming jealousy and insecurity takes time and effort. It is a journey of self-discovery and growth, both individually and as a couple. By implementing these strategies and seeking support when needed, you can create a foundation of trust, security, and love within your relationship.

11.2 Managing External Influences and Interference

External influences and interference can pose significant challenges to any relationship. Whether it's the opinions and judgments of friends and family, societal expectations, or even past experiences, these external factors can create tension and strain on the bond between partners. In order to overcome these obstacles and maintain a strong and healthy relationship, it is crucial to develop effective strategies for managing external influences.

11.2.1 Understanding the Impact of External Influences

External influences can come in various forms and have a profound impact on relationships. One common challenge is the interference of friends and family. While their intentions may be well-meaning, their opinions and judgments can often cloud the couple's judgment and create unnecessary conflicts. It is important to recognize that while loved ones may have their own perspectives, ultimately, the decisions and choices in a relationship should be made by the individuals involved.

Societal expectations can also play a significant role in influencing relationships. Society often imposes certain norms and standards that may not align with the unique dynamics and needs of a particular couple. It is essential to challenge these societal expectations and prioritize the authenticity and happiness of the relationship over external pressures.

Past experiences can also shape how individuals perceive and navigate relationships. Previous traumas or heartbreaks may create fear, insecurity, or trust issues that can hinder the growth and progress of a current relationship. It is crucial for both partners to acknowledge and address these past experiences in order to heal and move forward together.

11.2.2 Establishing Boundaries and Communication

One of the most effective ways to manage external influences and interference is by establishing clear boundaries and open communication within the relationship. By setting boundaries, couples can protect their relationship from external pressures and ensure that their needs and values are respected.

Open and honest communication is key in navigating external influences. Partners should feel comfortable expressing their concerns, fears, and desires to each other. By openly discussing the impact of external influences, couples can work together to find solutions and strategies that strengthen their bond.

11.2.3 Seeking Support and Guidance

Sometimes, managing external influences and interference can be challenging on your own. In such cases, seeking support and guidance from trusted sources can be immensely helpful. This could involve seeking professional counseling or therapy, joining support groups, or even reaching out to mentors or couples who have successfully navigated similar challenges.

Professional counselors or therapists can provide valuable insights and tools to help couples effectively manage external influences. They can offer guidance on how to communicate effectively, set boundaries, and address any underlying issues that may be contributing to the challenges faced.

Support groups can also provide a safe space for individuals to share their experiences and learn from others who have faced similar external influences. Connecting with others who have gone through similar struggles can offer validation, support, and practical advice.

11.2.4 Strengthening the Relationship

Ultimately, the strength of a relationship lies in the bond between the partners. By focusing on building a strong foundation and nurturing the connection between each other, couples can better withstand external influences and interference.

Investing time and effort into activities that promote emotional intimacy and connection is crucial. This could involve engaging in shared hobbies, going on regular date nights, or simply spending quality time together. By prioritizing the relationship and making it a priority, couples can create a solid foundation that is resilient to external pressures.

11.2.5 Embracing Individuality and Autonomy

While managing external influences is important, it is equally crucial to embrace individuality and autonomy within the relationship. Each partner should have the freedom to pursue their own interests, passions, and personal growth. By supporting each other's individuality, couples can strengthen their bond and create a sense of security and trust.

It is important to strike a balance between togetherness and independence. By finding a healthy equilibrium, couples can navigate external influences while still maintaining a strong sense of self and personal fulfillment.

In conclusion, managing external influences and interference is a vital aspect of maintaining a healthy and lasting relationship. By understanding the impact of external factors, establishing boundaries, seeking support, and nurturing the bond between partners, couples can overcome these challenges and create a relationship that thrives despite external pressures. Remember, the power to build a strong and resilient relationship lies within you and your partner.

11.3 Addressing Differences in Values and Beliefs

In any relationship, it is inevitable that there will be differences in values and beliefs between partners. These differences can arise from various factors such as cultural backgrounds, upbringing, personal experiences, and individual perspectives. While some differences can add depth and richness to a relationship, others can create challenges and conflicts if not addressed and managed effectively.

11.3.1 Understanding the Impact of Differences in Values and Beliefs

Values and beliefs are deeply ingrained in individuals and shape their thoughts, behaviors, and decision-making processes. They serve as guiding principles that influence how individuals perceive the world, make choices, and interact with others. When partners have conflicting values and beliefs, it can lead to misunderstandings, disagreements, and even resentment.

Differences in values and beliefs can manifest in various areas of a relationship, including:

1. **Religion and spirituality:** Varying religious or spiritual beliefs can impact how partners approach life's challenges, find meaning, and seek guidance. Conflicts may arise when partners have different religious practices or when one partner is more devout than the other.
2. **Politics and social issues:** Divergent political ideologies and opinions on social issues can create tension and heated debates within a relationship. Disagreements may arise regarding topics such as social justice, equality, and government policies.
3. **Family and parenting:** Varied beliefs about family dynamics, parenting styles, and the role of extended family members can lead to conflicts and challenges in creating a cohesive family unit. Differences in values regarding discipline, education, and cultural traditions may require open communication and compromise.
4. **Career and ambition:** Conflicting values regarding career aspirations,

work-life balance, and financial priorities can strain a relationship. Partners may have different levels of ambition or prioritize different aspects of their professional lives, leading to potential conflicts and resentment.

5. **Lifestyle choices:** Differences in values and beliefs regarding lifestyle choices such as diet, exercise, recreational activities, and personal habits can impact a relationship. Conflicts may arise when partners have contrasting preferences or expectations in these areas.

11.3.2 Open and Respectful Communication

Addressing differences in values and beliefs requires open and respectful communication between partners. It is essential to create a safe space where both individuals can express their thoughts, feelings, and perspectives without fear of judgment or rejection. Here are some strategies to facilitate effective communication:

1. **Active listening:** Practice active listening by giving your partner your full attention, maintaining eye contact, and showing genuine interest in their perspective. Avoid interrupting or formulating counterarguments while they are speaking.

2. **Empathy and understanding:** Seek to understand your partner's values and beliefs by putting yourself in their shoes. Show empathy and validate their experiences, even if you don't agree with their viewpoint.

3. **Clarification and reflection:** Clarify any misunderstandings by paraphrasing and reflecting back what your partner has shared. This demonstrates that you are actively engaged in the conversation and committed to understanding their perspective.

4. **Finding common ground:** Look for areas of shared values and beliefs to build upon. Identify common goals and aspirations that can serve as a foundation for compromise and collaboration.

5. **Respectful disagreement:** It is natural to have differing opinions, but it is crucial to express disagreement respectfully. Avoid personal attacks or

belittling your partner's beliefs. Instead, focus on discussing the specific issue at hand and finding common ground.

11.3.3 Seeking Compromise and Collaboration

When faced with differences in values and beliefs, it is essential to find ways to bridge the gap and seek compromise. Here are some strategies to foster compromise and collaboration:

1. **Open-mindedness:** Approach the situation with an open mind and a willingness to consider alternative perspectives. Recognize that there may be multiple valid ways of viewing a situation.
2. **Flexibility:** Be willing to adapt and adjust your own beliefs and behaviors when necessary. Recognize that compromise often involves finding middle ground rather than one person completely giving in to the other.
3. **Negotiation:** Engage in constructive negotiation to find solutions that honor both partners' values and beliefs. Look for creative alternatives that can meet both individuals' needs to the best extent possible.
4. **Shared values exploration:** Take the time to explore and understand each other's values more deeply. Discuss the underlying reasons behind your respective beliefs and identify shared values that can serve as a foundation for compromise.
5. **Professional support:** In some cases, seeking the guidance of a relationship counselor or therapist can be beneficial. A trained professional can provide tools and techniques to navigate differences in values and beliefs and facilitate productive conversations.

11.3.4 Embracing Growth and Learning

Addressing differences in values and beliefs requires a growth mindset and a commitment to ongoing learning. It is essential to recognize that relationships evolve and change over time, and so do individuals' values and beliefs. Here are some ways to embrace growth and learning:

1. **Self-reflection:** Continuously reflect on your own values and beliefs, and be open to reevaluating and evolving them as you gain new experiences and insights. This self-awareness can contribute to personal growth and a deeper understanding of your partner.
2. **Education and exposure:** Seek opportunities to learn about different cultures, religions, and perspectives. Engage in activities that broaden your understanding of the world and challenge your preconceived notions.
3. **Shared learning:** Engage in joint activities that promote learning and growth as a couple. Attend workshops, seminars, or classes together on topics related to values, beliefs, and personal development.
4. **Mutual respect:** Foster an environment of mutual respect where both partners feel safe to express their evolving values and beliefs. Encourage open dialogue and celebrate each other's growth and learning journeys.
5. **Adaptability:** Recognize that as individuals and as a couple, you will encounter new experiences and challenges that may shape your values and beliefs. Embrace the opportunity to adapt and grow together, knowing that change is a natural part of life and relationships.

By addressing differences in values and beliefs with open communication, compromise, and a commitment to growth, couples can navigate these challenges and build a strong foundation for a lasting and fulfilling relationship. Remember that differences can be an opportunity for growth and understanding, and with the right skills and mindset, couples can overcome these obstacles and create a love that thrives on mutual respect and shared values.

11.4 Working Through Trauma and Past Baggage

Trauma and past baggage can have a significant impact on our ability to form and maintain healthy relationships. Many lesbians and queer women have experienced various forms of trauma, including discrimination, rejection, and even violence, which can leave deep emotional scars. These experiences can create barriers to intimacy and trust, making it challenging to build and sustain a lasting love.

Understanding the Impact of Trauma

Trauma can manifest in different ways and affect individuals in unique ways. It is essential to recognize that trauma is not a reflection of personal weakness or failure but rather a natural response to overwhelming experiences. Traumatic events can range from childhood abuse or neglect to adult experiences of discrimination, homophobia, or relationship violence.

When trauma is left unaddressed, it can have a profound impact on our relationships. It can lead to difficulties in trusting others, fear of vulnerability, and a tendency to push people away. Trauma can also contribute to emotional reactivity, hypervigilance, and difficulties with emotional regulation. These challenges can make it challenging to establish and maintain healthy connections with others.

Healing from Trauma

Working through trauma and past baggage is a crucial step towards creating a lasting love. It requires a commitment to self-care, self-reflection, and seeking support from trusted professionals or support groups. Here are some strategies that can help in the healing process:

11.4.1 Seeking Professional Help

Therapy can be a valuable resource for individuals who have experienced trauma. A skilled therapist can provide a safe and supportive environment to explore and process past experiences. They can help identify patterns, develop coping strategies, and work towards healing and growth. Trauma-focused therapies, such as Eye Movement Desensitization and Reprocessing (EMDR) or Cognitive-Behavioral Therapy (CBT), can be particularly effective in addressing trauma-related challenges.

11.4.2 Building a Support Network

Connecting with others who have experienced similar traumas can be incredibly healing. Support groups or community organizations can provide a sense of belonging, validation, and understanding. Sharing experiences and learning from others who have navigated similar challenges can be empowering and help in the healing process.

11.4.3 Practicing Self-Care

Self-care is essential for healing from trauma. Engaging in activities that promote relaxation, self-compassion, and self-expression can help restore a sense of well-being. This may include practices such as mindfulness, journaling, creative outlets, physical exercise, or spending time in nature. Taking care of your physical, emotional, and mental health is crucial in building resilience and creating a foundation for healthy relationships.

11.4.4 Developing Emotional Awareness

Trauma can disrupt our ability to identify and regulate our emotions. Developing emotional awareness is a vital skill in healing from past trauma. This involves learning to recognize and understand our emotions, as well as finding healthy ways to express and process them. Mindfulness practices, therapy, and self-reflection can all contribute to developing emotional awareness and fostering emotional resilience.

11.4.5 Communicating Boundaries and Needs

Trauma can impact our ability to establish and communicate boundaries effectively. It is crucial to learn how to assertively communicate our needs and boundaries in relationships. This involves developing clear and open communication skills, as well as learning to advocate for ourselves. Setting boundaries is an essential part of creating a safe and secure environment for both partners in a relationship.

Moving Forward

Working through trauma and past baggage is a journey that requires patience, self-compassion, and a commitment to personal growth. It is essential to remember that healing is possible and that you deserve love and happiness. By seeking support, practicing self-care, and developing healthy relationship skills, you can overcome the obstacles that trauma may present and create a lasting love built on trust, understanding, and mutual respect.

Remember, healing takes time, and it is okay to seek professional help or support from others along the way. You are not alone, and there are resources available to help you navigate the healing process. With dedication and self-love, you can overcome the challenges of trauma and build a fulfilling and lasting love.

12

Chapter 12

12.Creating a Lasting Love

12.1 Practicing Gratitude and Appreciation

In the journey of creating a lasting love, one of the most powerful tools you can utilize is the practice of gratitude and appreciation. When we express gratitude and appreciation towards our partner, we not only strengthen the bond between us but also cultivate a positive and loving atmosphere within our relationship. This practice has the potential to transform the way we perceive and experience love.

The Power of Gratitude

Gratitude is a practice that involves acknowledging and appreciating the blessings, big and small, that we have in our lives. When we extend this practice to our relationships, it allows us to focus on the positive aspects of our partner and the love we share. By consciously recognizing and expressing gratitude for the qualities, actions, and efforts of our partner, we create a foundation of appreciation that can strengthen our connection.

Gratitude has the power to shift our perspective from what may be lacking in our relationship to what is abundant and fulfilling. It helps us to cultivate a mindset of abundance and contentment, rather than one of scarcity and dissatisfaction. When we approach our relationship with gratitude, we are more likely to notice and cherish the moments of joy, love, and support that our partner brings into our lives.

Expressing Appreciation

Appreciation is the act of recognizing and valuing the qualities, actions, and contributions of our partner. It involves expressing our gratitude and admiration for who they are and what they bring to the relationship. Appreciation can be expressed through words, gestures, or acts of kindness that communicate our love and admiration.

When we express appreciation, we not only uplift our partner but also strengthen the emotional bond between us. It creates a positive feedback loop where both partners feel seen, valued, and loved. By acknowledging and appreciating the efforts and qualities of our partner, we create an environment of mutual respect and support.

Cultivating a Gratitude Practice

To incorporate gratitude and appreciation into your relationship, consider the following practices:

1. Daily Gratitude Ritual: Set aside a few moments each day to reflect on and express gratitude for your partner. This can be done through journaling, sharing your appreciation verbally, or even writing a heartfelt note. Focus on specific qualities, actions, or moments that you are grateful for.

2. Appreciation Dates: Plan special dates or moments dedicated to expressing appreciation for each other. This can involve taking turns sharing what you appreciate about one another or surprising your partner with gestures that show your admiration and love.

3. Gratitude Jar: Create a gratitude jar where both partners can write down moments of gratitude and appreciation. Whenever you or your partner need a reminder of the love and appreciation in your relationship, you can revisit these notes and relive those cherished moments.

4. Mindful Communication: Practice active listening and validation when your partner expresses their thoughts, feelings, or experiences. Show genuine interest and appreciation for their perspective, even if it differs from your own. This fosters a sense of understanding and deepens the connection between you.

5. Random Acts of Kindness: Surprise your partner with small acts of kindness and appreciation. It could be as simple as preparing their favorite meal, leaving a heartfelt note, or offering a comforting gesture when they are feeling down. These acts of love and appreciation can have a profound impact on the overall happiness and satisfaction within your relationship.

Remember, the practice of gratitude and appreciation is not a one-time event but an ongoing commitment to nurturing and cherishing your relationship. By incorporating these practices into your daily life, you create a foundation of love, respect, and gratitude that can sustain and deepen your connection over time.

In the next section, we will explore the concept of fostering a growth mindset in relationships, which complements the practice of gratitude and appreciation in creating a lasting love.

12.2 Fostering a Growth Mindset in Relationships

In order to foster a growth mindset in relationships, it is important to understand that personal growth and development are ongoing processes. Just as individuals continue to learn and evolve throughout their lives, relationships also require continuous learning and growth to thrive. By adopting a growth mindset, you can cultivate an environment of growth, understanding, and resilience within your relationship.

12.2.1 Embracing Change and Adaptability

One of the key aspects of fostering a growth mindset in relationships is embracing change and adaptability. Relationships, like individuals, go through different stages and phases. It is important to recognize that change is inevitable and that both partners will evolve and grow over time. By embracing change and being open to adapting to new circumstances, you can navigate the challenges and transitions that arise in your relationship with greater ease.

12.2.2 Emphasizing Communication and Feedback

Effective communication is essential for fostering a growth mindset in relationships. It is important to create a safe and open space where both partners can express their thoughts, feelings, and needs. By actively listening to each other and providing constructive feedback, you can foster a sense of understanding and empathy within your relationship. This allows for continuous growth and improvement as you learn from each other's perspectives and experiences.

12.2.3 Cultivating a Learning Attitude

A growth mindset in relationships involves cultivating a learning attitude. This means being open to new ideas, perspectives, and experiences. It is important to approach challenges and conflicts as opportunities for growth and learning rather than as obstacles. By viewing setbacks as learning experiences, you can develop resilience and find creative solutions to problems that arise in your relationship.

12.2.4 Embracing Vulnerability and Authenticity

Vulnerability and authenticity are essential components of a growth mindset in relationships. It is important to create a safe and non-judgmental space where both partners can be their true selves. By being vulnerable and sharing your fears, insecurities, and desires, you can deepen your emotional connection and foster a sense of intimacy. This allows for personal growth and encourages your partner to do the same.

12.2.5 Encouraging Personal Development

Fostering a growth mindset in relationships involves encouraging personal development for both partners. This means supporting each other's goals, passions, and interests. By nurturing individual growth, you can create a strong foundation for the growth of your relationship. Encourage each other to pursue personal goals, engage in self-reflection, and engage in activities that promote personal growth and self-improvement.

12.2.6 Emphasizing Gratitude and Appreciation

Practicing gratitude and appreciation is a powerful way to foster a growth mindset in relationships. By expressing gratitude for the positive aspects of your relationship and appreciating each other's efforts, you can create a positive and nurturing environment. This cultivates a sense of mutual respect and encourages both partners to continue growing and improving.

12.2.7 Seeking Support and Resources

Fostering a growth mindset in relationships also involves seeking support and utilizing available resources. This can include attending relationship workshops, reading books on relationships, or seeking guidance from a relationship coach or therapist. By actively seeking support and utilizing resources, you can gain valuable insights and tools to further enhance your relationship growth.

12.2.8 Embracing the Journey

Finally, fostering a growth mindset in relationships requires embracing the journey. Recognize that personal growth and relationship growth are ongoing processes that require time, effort, and patience. Embrace the ups and downs, the challenges and triumphs, and the continuous learning that comes with being in a relationship. By embracing the journey, you can create a lasting love that continues to evolve and thrive.

Remember, fostering a growth mindset in relationships is a choice that requires commitment and effort from both partners. By embracing change, emphasizing communication, cultivating a learning attitude, embracing vulnerability, encouraging personal development, emphasizing gratitude, seeking support, and embracing the journey, you can create a relationship that is resilient, fulfilling, and continuously evolving.

12.3 Committing to Lifelong Learning and Growth

In order to create a lasting love, it is essential to commit to lifelong learning and growth within your relationship. Relationships are dynamic and ever-evolving, and it is crucial to continuously develop and refine your skills to navigate the challenges and changes that may arise.

12.3.1 Embracing a Growth Mindset

One of the key aspects of committing to lifelong learning and growth is embracing a growth mindset. A growth mindset is the belief that abilities and qualities can be developed through dedication and hard work. By adopting a growth mindset, you open yourself up to new possibilities and opportunities for personal and relational growth.

In the context of a relationship, a growth mindset allows you to approach challenges and setbacks as opportunities for learning and improvement. Instead of viewing difficulties as insurmountable obstacles, you see them as chances to deepen your understanding of yourself and your partner. This mindset fosters resilience, adaptability, and a willingness to put in the effort required to nurture a lasting love.

12.3.2 Cultivating Curiosity and Openness

Another important aspect of lifelong learning and growth in relationships is cultivating curiosity and openness. Curiosity involves a genuine interest in understanding your partner's thoughts, feelings, and experiences. It is about asking questions, actively listening, and seeking to learn more about each other on an ongoing basis.

Openness, on the other hand, involves being receptive to new ideas, perspectives, and feedback. It means being willing to challenge your own assumptions and beliefs, and being open to personal growth and change. By cultivating curiosity and openness, you create a space for continuous learning and growth within your relationship.

12.3.3 Seeking Knowledge and Resources

Committing to lifelong learning and growth also means actively seeking knowledge and resources to enhance your relationship skills. There are numerous books, workshops, courses, and therapists available that can provide valuable insights and tools for building a lasting love.

Reading books on relationships, attending workshops or seminars, and seeking guidance from relationship experts can offer new perspectives and practical strategies for navigating challenges and fostering a deeper connection with your partner. It is important to approach these resources with an open mind and a willingness to integrate new ideas and practices into your relationship.

12.3.4 Practicing Self-Reflection and Self-Awareness

Self-reflection and self-awareness are essential components of lifelong learning and growth in relationships. Taking the time to reflect on your own thoughts, feelings, and behaviors allows you to gain insight into how you contribute to the dynamics of your relationship.

By developing self-awareness, you can identify patterns, triggers, and areas for personal growth. This self-awareness enables you to take responsibility for your own actions and reactions, and make conscious choices that align with your values and relationship goals.

12.3.5 Embracing Feedback and Communication

Feedback and communication are vital for ongoing learning and growth in relationships. Creating a safe and open environment where both partners can express their thoughts, feelings, and needs without fear of judgment or criticism is crucial.

By actively seeking and embracing feedback from your partner, you can gain valuable insights into areas where you can improve and grow. Effective communication skills, such as active listening, empathy, and nonviolent communication techniques, facilitate open and honest dialogue, fostering a deeper understanding and connection between you and your partner.

12.3.6 Emphasizing Personal and Relationship Goals

Committing to lifelong learning and growth involves setting personal and relationship goals. These goals provide a sense of direction and purpose, and serve as a roadmap for ongoing development and improvement.

Personal goals may include areas such as self-care, self-improvement, and personal growth. Relationship goals, on the other hand, focus on enhancing the connection, intimacy, and overall satisfaction within the partnership. By regularly revisiting and reassessing these goals, you can ensure that you are both actively working towards a shared vision of a lasting love.

12.3.7 Embracing Change and Adaptability

Lastly, committing to lifelong learning and growth in relationships requires embracing change and adaptability. Relationships are not static; they evolve and transform over time. By being open to change and adaptable in the face of new circumstances, you can navigate the ups and downs of life together with resilience and grace.

Embracing change also means being willing to let go of old patterns, beliefs, and behaviors that no longer serve you or your relationship. It involves being open to new experiences, perspectives, and ways of being, allowing your relationship to grow and flourish.

In conclusion, committing to lifelong learning and growth is essential for creating a lasting love. By embracing a growth mindset, cultivating curiosity and openness, seeking knowledge and resources, practicing self-reflection and self-awareness, embracing feedback and communication, emphasizing personal and relationship goals, and embracing change and adaptability, you can continuously develop and refine your relationship skills. Remember, a happy, healthy, and lasting relationship is within your reach once you commit to lifelong learning and growth.

12.4 Building a Legacy of Love and Connection

Building a lasting love and connection is not just about the present moment; it is about creating a legacy that will endure for years to come. It is about leaving a mark on the world through the love and connection you cultivate in your relationship. In this section, we will explore the importance of building a legacy of love and connection and provide practical strategies to help you achieve this goal.

12.4.1 The Power of Love and Connection

Love and connection have the power to transform not only our individual lives but also the world around us. When we prioritize love and connection in our relationships, we create a ripple effect that extends far beyond ourselves. Our love and connection become a source of inspiration and support for others, encouraging them to seek and cultivate their own meaningful relationships.

Love and connection also have the power to heal. They can heal past wounds, mend broken hearts, and provide solace in times of hardship. By building a legacy of love and connection, we contribute to the healing of ourselves, our partners, and the wider community.

12.4.2 Leaving a Lasting Impact

Building a legacy of love and connection means leaving a lasting impact on the lives of those we love. It means creating a relationship that is not only fulfilling in the present but also serves as a foundation for future generations. When we prioritize love and connection, we create a relationship that becomes a source of strength and inspiration for our children, grandchildren, and beyond.

Leaving a lasting impact also means being intentional about the values and principles we pass on to future generations. By cultivating a relationship based on love, respect, and empathy, we create a blueprint for future relationships to thrive. Our legacy becomes a testament to the power of love and connection in creating a better world.

12.4.3 Nurturing Love and Connection

To build a legacy of love and connection, it is essential to nurture and cultivate these qualities in our relationship. Here are some strategies to help you on this journey:

12.4.3.1 Cultivate a Culture of Appreciation

Expressing gratitude and appreciation for your partner is a powerful way to nurture love and connection. Take the time to acknowledge and celebrate the qualities and actions that you admire in your partner. By creating a culture of appreciation, you foster an environment of love and positivity in your relationship.

12.4.3.2 Practice Active Listening

Active listening is a skill that allows you to truly understand and empathize with your partner. Make a conscious effort to listen attentively, without interrupting or judging. Show genuine interest in your partner's thoughts, feelings, and experiences. By practicing active listening, you create a safe space for open and honest communication, deepening your connection.

12.4.3.3 Continual Growth and Learning

Commit to lifelong learning and growth as individuals and as a couple. Seek opportunities for personal development, whether it be through reading books, attending workshops, or engaging in therapy. By investing in your personal growth, you bring new insights and perspectives into your relationship, fostering a sense of growth and vitality.

12.4.3.4 Create Rituals and Traditions

Rituals and traditions provide a sense of stability and continuity in a relationship. Establish meaningful rituals that you can engage in regularly, such as date nights, family dinners, or annual vacations. These rituals create a sense of belonging and togetherness, strengthening your bond and creating lasting memories.

12.4.3.5 Give Back to the Community

Building a legacy of love and connection extends beyond your immediate relationship. Find ways to give back to your community together. Volunteer for a cause you both care about, participate in charitable events, or support local organizations. By contributing to the well-being of others, you deepen your connection and leave a positive impact on the world.

12.4.4 Embracing the Journey

Building a legacy of love and connection is not a destination; it is a lifelong journey. Embrace the ups and downs, the challenges and triumphs, knowing that each experience contributes to the growth and strength of your relationship. Remember that love and connection require effort and intentionality, but the rewards are immeasurable.

As you embark on this journey, keep in mind that building a legacy of love and connection is not about perfection. It is about showing up authentically, being vulnerable, and continuously striving to be the best version of yourself. By doing so, you create a relationship that not only stands the test of time but also inspires others to cultivate their own legacy of love and connection.

Remember, you have the power to create a lasting love and connection that will leave a positive impact on the world. Embrace this opportunity and build a legacy that will be cherished for generations to come.